ROMUALDO

gua®

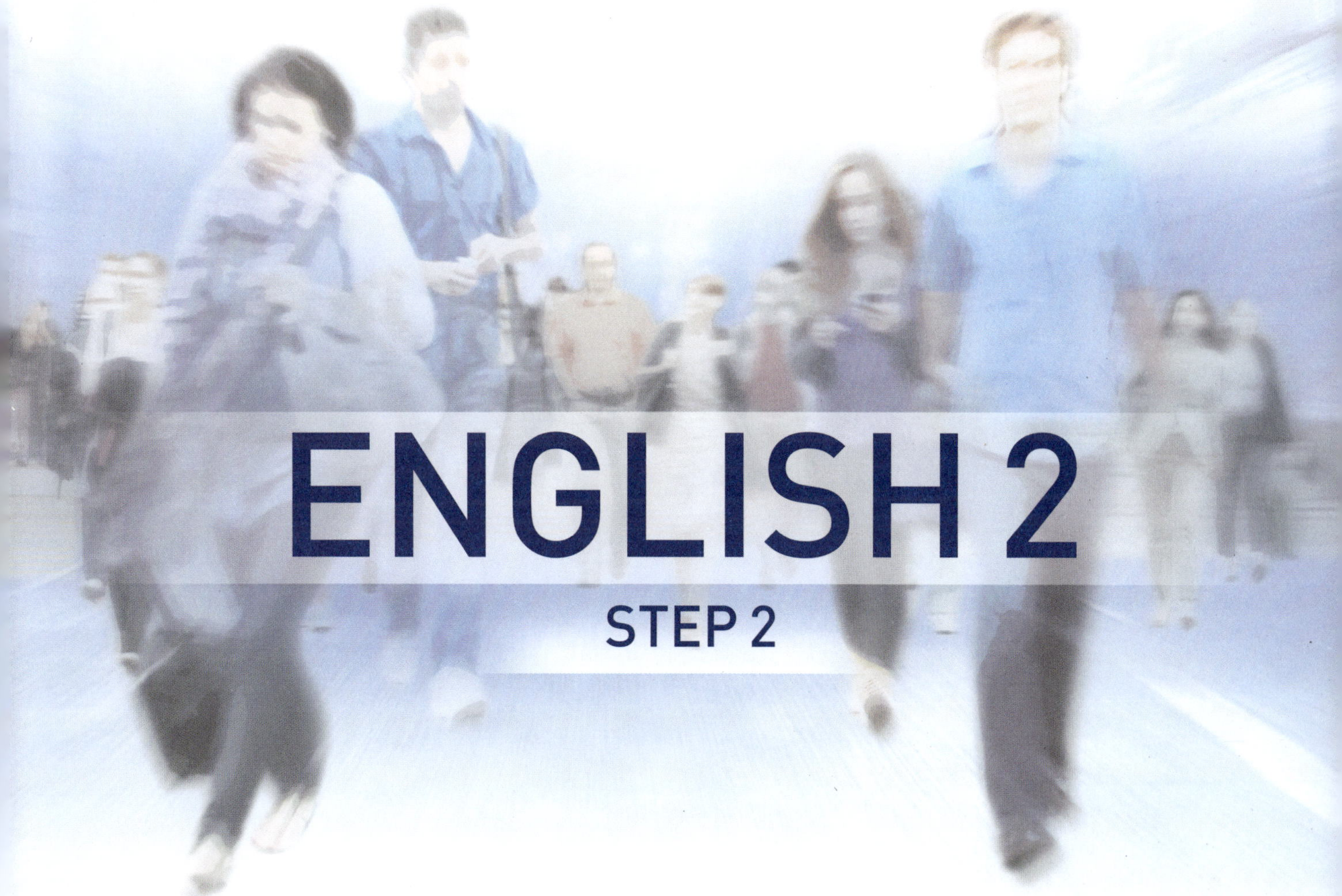

ENGLISH 2

STEP 2

Impressum

Published by inlingua International Ltd., Bern, Switzerland
For the exclusive use of inlingua language centers

www.inlingua.com
comments@inlingua.com

© 2012 by inlingua International Ltd., Bern, Switzerland

First published 2012
4th edition 2018

Design, Layout and Cartoons by Stämpfli Ltd., Bern
Printed and bound by CPI books, Ulm, Germany

Pictures:
© dreamstime.com, © fotolia.com, © iStockphoto.com, © cinetext.de
© shutterstock.com, © keystone.com, © depositphoto.com
and by Stämpfli Publications Ltd., Bern

Item number e2210

Welcome to English 2 Step 2

Step-by-step to perfect communication

English 2 Step 2 is part of the English language learning program published by inlingua International. It has been carefully designed for use with the inlingua language training method.

The wide range of contemporary topics and practical issues makes the Course Book challenging and motivating. The attractive, user-friendly layout and progressive language content will help you develop the speaking, listening, reading and writing skills needed to communicate effectively in today's international environment.

English 2 Step 1 and Step 2 will take you to level B1 of the Common European Framework of Reference for Languages (CEFR) or US level 1+ of the Interagency Language Roundtable (ILR).

Overview of inlingua and international levels

inlingua English Program	CEFR levels	ILR
5 Step 2 5 Step 1	C2	4+ 4
4 Step 2 4 Step 1	C1	3+ 3
3 Step 2 3 Step 1	B2	2+ 2
2 Step 2 2 Step 1	B1	1+ 1
1 Step 2 1 Step 1	A2 A1	1 0+

mp3 audio download

https://www.inlingua.com/audios/

Table of Contents

Unit 16 Reactions   1

16.1 Discussing opinions
16.2 Agreeing and disagreeing
16.3 Reporting comments and views

Reading **1** / Listening **3** / Follow-up **4**
Language Summary **5** / Talking Point **6**

Unit 17 On the Phone   7

17.1 Talking about telephoning
17.2 Getting through on the phone
17.3 Reporting information

Reading **7** / Listening **9** / Follow-up **10**
Language Summary **11** / Talking Point **12**

Unit 18 In Control   13

18.1 Talking about electrical devices
18.2 Understanding simple technical instructions
18.3 Describing controlling actions

Reading **13** / Listening **15** / Follow-up **16**
Language Summary **17** / Talking Point **18**

Unit 19 Shelter   19

19.1 Describing building interiors
19.2 Describing building exteriors
19.3 Describing designs

Reading **19** / Listening **21** / Follow-up **22**
Language Summary **23** / Talking Point **24**

Unit 20 Hard Work   25

20.1 Discussing everyday tasks
20.2 Describing and comparing actions
20.3 Describing past routines

Reading **25** / Listening **27** / Follow-up **28**
Language Summary **29** / Talking Point **30**

Units 16–20 Summary   31

Grammar Summary **31**
Vocabulary Summary **33**
Skills Summary **34**

Table of Contents

Unit 21 Problems   35

21.1 Discussing problems and difficulties
21.2 Making and responding to suggestions
21.3 Discussing past problems and solutions

Reading 35 / Listening 37 / Follow-up 38
Language Summary 39 / Talking Point 40

Unit 22 People and Places   41

22.1 Discussing social issues
22.2 Referring to places, people and things
22.3 Discussing city attractions

Reading 41 / Listening 43 / Follow-up 44
Language Summary 45 / Talking Point 46

Unit 23 Culture   47

23.1 Using polite expressions
23.2 Asking questions politely
23.3 Describing personalities

Reading 47 / Listening 49 / Follow-up 50
Language Summary 51 / Talking Point 52

Unit 24 Eating Out   53

24.1 Talking about places to eat
24.2 Talking about menus
24.3 Using polite language at the table

Reading 53 / Listening 55 / Follow-up 56
Language Summary 57 / Talking Point 58

Unit 25 Consumer Society   59

25.1 Understanding advertisements
25.2 Discussing precautions
25.3 Describing trends

Reading 59 / Listening 61 / Follow-up 62
Language Summary 63 / Talking Point 64

Units 21–25 Summary   65

Grammar Summary 65
Vocabulary Summary 67
Skills Summary 68

Table of Contents

Unit 26 Money   69

26.1 Discussing money matters
26.2 Discussing money matters in the past
26.3 Giving precise and approximate figures

Reading **69** / Listening **71** / Follow-up **72**
Language Summary **73** / Talking Point **74**

Unit 27 Emotions   75

27.1 Describing positive feelings
27.2 Describing negative feelings
27.3 Linking and contrasting

Reading **75** / Listening **77** / Follow-up **78**
Language Summary **79** / Talking Point **80**

Unit 28 Entertainment   81

28.1 Talking about TV programs
28.2 Talking about music
28.3 Talking about stories

Reading **81** / Listening **83** / Follow-up **84**
Language Summary **85** / Talking Point **86**

Unit 29 Enjoy Your Stay   87

29.1 Talking about tourist accommodations
29.2 Making accommodation arrangements
29.3 Discussing faults and problems

Reading **87** / Listening **89** / Follow-up **90**
Language Summary **91** / Talking Point **92**

Unit 30 The Big Picture   93

30.1 Describing directions and movement
30.2 Explaining causes and effects
30.3 Discussing certain and uncertain information

Reading **93** / Listening **95** / Follow-up **96**
Language Summary **97** / Talking Point **98**

Units 26–30 Summary   99

Grammar Summary **99**
Vocabulary Summary **101**
Skills Summary **102**

Language Practice   103

Extra Practice   115

Listening Texts   131

Solutions   141

Irregular Verbs   159

Index   161

Maps   177

UNIT 16
REACTIONS

16.1 Discussing opinions
16.2 Agreeing and disagreeing
16.3 Reporting comments and views

16.1 Reading

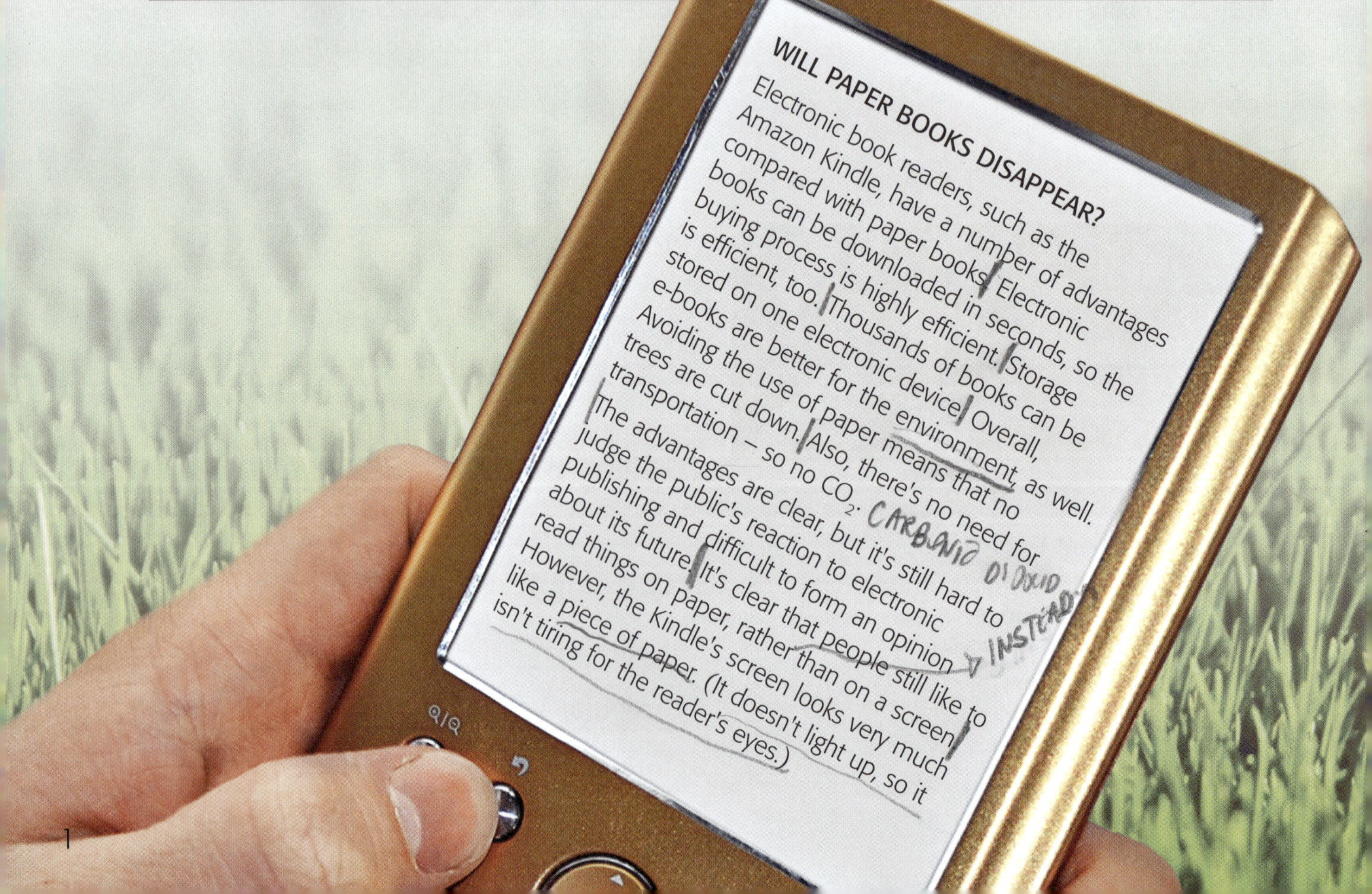

WILL PAPER BOOKS DISAPPEAR?

Electronic book readers, such as the Amazon Kindle, have a number of advantages compared with paper books. Electronic books can be downloaded in seconds, so the buying process is highly efficient. The storage is efficient, too. Thousands of books can be stored on one electronic device. Overall, e-books are better for the environment, as well. Avoiding the use of paper means that trees are cut down. Also, there's no need for transportation – so no CO_2. CARBONIO DI OSSID

The advantages are clear, but it's still hard to judge the public's reaction to electronic publishing and difficult to form an opinion about its future. It's clear that people still like to read things on paper, rather than on a screen INSTEAD. However, the Kindle's screen looks very much like a piece of paper. (It doesn't light up, so it isn't tiring for the reader's eyes.)

16.2 Reading

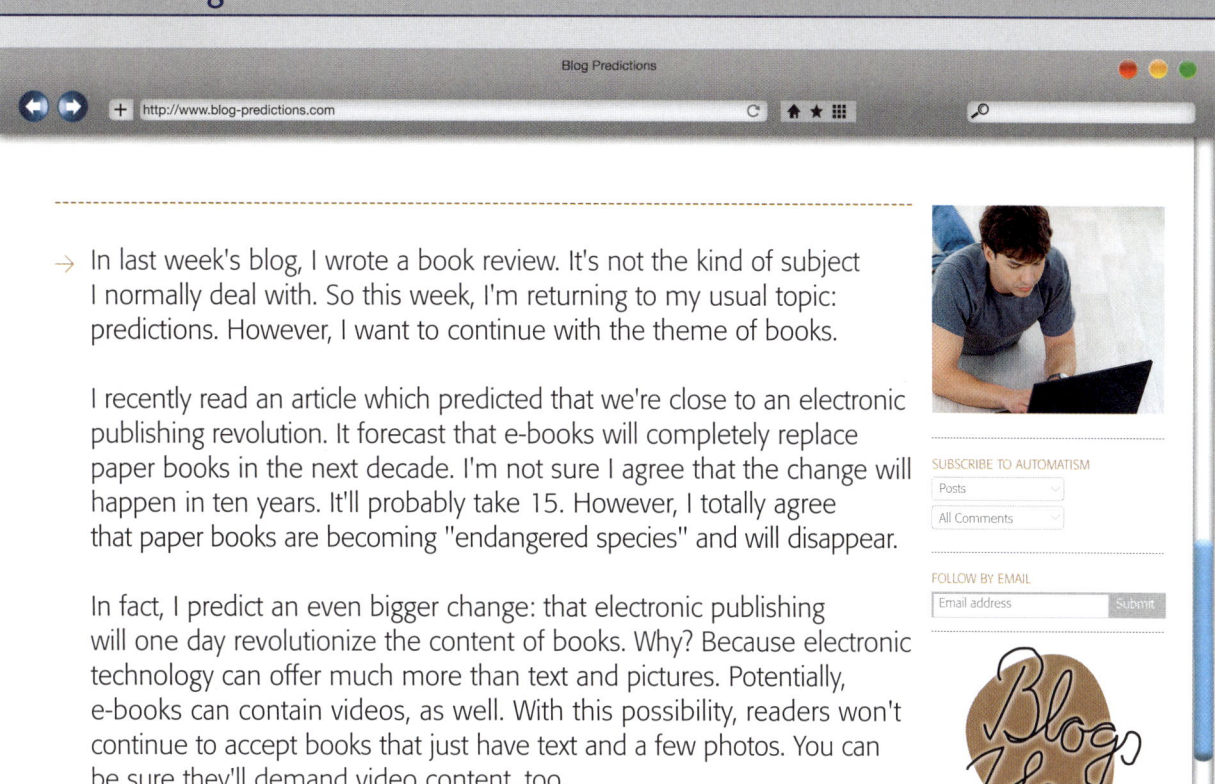

In last week's blog, I wrote a book review. It's not the kind of subject I normally deal with. So this week, I'm returning to my usual topic: predictions. However, I want to continue with the theme of books.

I recently read an article which predicted that we're close to an electronic publishing revolution. It forecast that e-books will completely replace paper books in the next decade. I'm not sure I agree that the change will happen in ten years. It'll probably take 15. However, I totally agree that paper books are becoming "endangered species" and will disappear.

In fact, I predict an even bigger change: that electronic publishing will one day revolutionize the content of books. Why? Because electronic technology can offer much more than text and pictures. Potentially, e-books can contain videos, as well. With this possibility, readers won't continue to accept books that just have text and a few photos. You can be sure they'll demand video content, too.

16.3 Reading

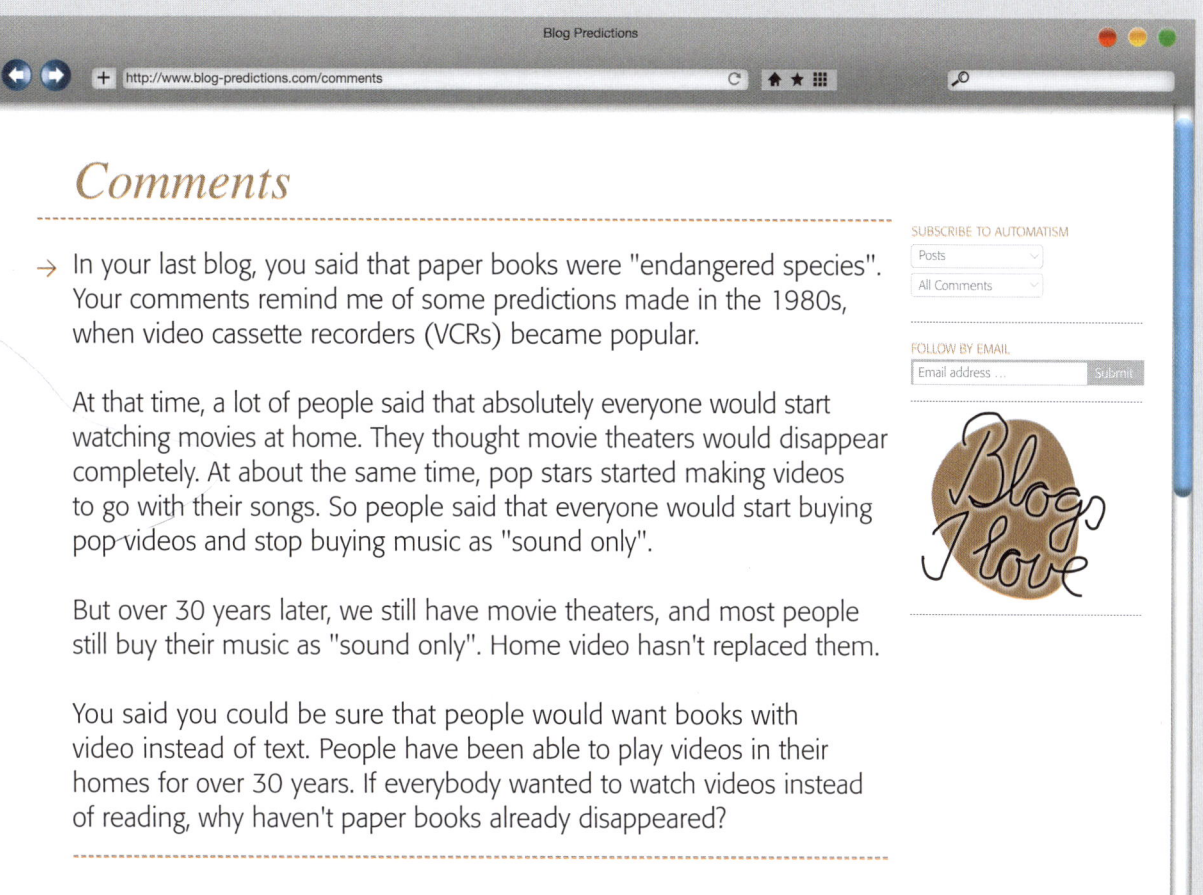

Comments

In your last blog, you said that paper books were "endangered species". Your comments remind me of some predictions made in the 1980s, when video cassette recorders (VCRs) became popular.

At that time, a lot of people said that absolutely everyone would start watching movies at home. They thought movie theaters would disappear completely. At about the same time, pop stars started making videos to go with their songs. So people said that everyone would start buying pop videos and stop buying music as "sound only".

But over 30 years later, we still have movie theaters, and most people still buy their music as "sound only". Home video hasn't replaced them.

You said you could be sure that people would want books with video instead of text. People have been able to play videos in their homes for over 30 years. If everybody wanted to watch videos instead of reading, why haven't paper books already disappeared?

16

16.1 Listening (Track 1)

Handwritten note: HOME WORK PG 103 (16.3) PG 4 (16.1/16.2/16.3)

Part A In a moment, you're going to hear an interview with a woman who reads lots of books. She discusses her opinions about the future of e-books. Try to complete the extracts from the interview, using the words below. Then, listen and check your answers.

~~opinion~~   say   ~~sure~~   ~~sure~~   ~~think~~   ~~think~~   ~~view~~

1 …I **THINK** the concept of electronic publishing is …
2 In my **OPINION**, e-books will definitely …
3 Although I'm not **SURE** whether electronic copies will …
4 I'd **SAY** we'll continue to have …
5 I'm **SURE** music will become …
6 But I don't **THINK** books will go in the same …
7 But that's just my point of **VIEW** (view). Maybe I'm …

Part B Listen again. Then, complete the ends of the sentences above in order to explain the woman's opinions. You can use your own words.

16.2 Listening (Track 2)

Part A You're going to hear a conversation between a man and the woman from Listening 16.1. They discuss their reactions to the views in the blog in Reading 16.2. Listen, then answer the questions below.

1 Does the woman agree or disagree with the blog?
2 Does the man agree or disagree with it?
3 What do they say about a lot of the texts that people publish on the web?

Part B Listen again. Complete the phrases for disagreeing from the conversation. Then rank the three phrases A–C in order of strength of disagreement.

A Well, I _____ agree that paper books are an "endangered species".
B Basically, I _____ disagree with everything in this blog.
C I'm _____ I agree that the change will happen in ten years.

Strongest ←——————————————————————— Weakest

Strength of disagreement _____ → _____ → _____

Part C In the conversation, there are four single words used to express agreement. Listen again and write down the four different words used.

1 _____   2 _____   3 _____   4 _____

16.3 Listening (Track 3)

Listen to five recordings of observations and predictions, from TV and radio programs in the 1980s. Write down what the people said.

1 She said *people would start buying all their music as pop videos*.
2 He said _____.
3 He said _____.
4 She said _____.
5 He said _____.

3

16.1 Follow-up

Write sentences about the advantages of electronic book readers next to the key words below. Then compare what you wrote with the information in the article in Reading 16.1.

1 buying
2 storage
3 environment
4 transportation

16.2 Follow-up

Look at the blog in Reading 16.2. Does the writer agree or disagree with the points below?

1 In the next ten years, paper books will disappear. A D
2 Paper books will eventually disappear. A D
3 Because of e-books, the content of books will change. A D
4 Future e-books will contain just text and photos. A D

16.3 Follow-up

Look at the comments in Reading 16.3, then answer the questions below.

1 Does the writer agree or disagree that paper books will disappear?

2 In the 1980s, what did some people predict about movie theaters?

3 What prediction did some people make about pop music in the 1980s?

4 In the writer's opinion, will the e-books of the future contain video?

5 What reason does the writer give for this opinion?

16.1 Language Summary — Discussing opinions

I think ▸ that's a good idea.
In my opinion, ▸ that's true.
I'd say

I'm sure that's a good idea.
I'm not sure (whether) that's true.

It's easy to use. ▸ It also looks good.
▸ It looks good, ▸ too.
▸ as well.

→ LANGUAGE PRACTICE 16.1 → PAGE 103

16.2 Language Summary — Agreeing and disagreeing

strong agreement
I totally agree.
I agree.
I'm not sure I agree.
I don't really agree.
I disagree.
strong disagreement
I totally disagree.

Do you think that's a good idea? – Yes. ▸ Sure.
▸ Definitely.
▸ Absolutely.

→ LANGUAGE PRACTICE 16.2 → PAGE 103

16.3 Language Summary — Reporting comments and views

What someone said	Saying what the person said
"I like the idea."	She said (that) she likes the idea.
	or She said (that) she liked the idea.
"I don't like the idea."	She said (that) she doesn't like the idea.
	or She said (that) she didn't like the idea.
"I'm working abroad."	She said (that) she's working abroad.
	or She said (that) she was working abroad.
"I can come to the meeting."	She said (that) she can come to the meeting.
	or She said (that) she could come to the meeting.
"I'll phone in a few weeks."	She said (that) she'll phone in a few weeks.
	or She said (that) she would phone in a few weeks.

→ LANGUAGE PRACTICE 16.3 → PAGE 103

Talking Point

Opinion, Expression and Culture

1
In a foreign language, expressing opinions can be difficult. Compared with simple two-way dialogues, such as buying tickets and ordering snacks, conversations about opinions are deeper – more three-dimensional. In fact, discussions about opinions also have a fourth dimension: culture. Culture doesn't just affect the views people have. It also affects the language they use to express their opinions, and to agree and disagree with one another's views.

2
Discuss how culture can affect the way people exchange opinions.

3
Look at the descriptions of cultural differences on the *Resource Sheet*. Compare them with the points you mentioned in your discussion.

4
Think about the points on the *Resource Sheet* and the issues you discussed. What lessons can be learned? What general advice would you give about discussing opinions, and agreeing and disagreeing, with people from other cultures?

UNIT 17
ON THE PHONE

17.1 Talking about telephoning
17.2 Getting through on the phone
17.3 Reporting information

17.1 Reading

Telecommunications is a fast-moving field, which means telephoning technology – and terminology – are constantly evolving. However, in English, the essential terms that describe making phone calls haven't changed since the telephone was invented. For non-native speakers, these words can be confusing. That's because they describe the operation of old-fashioned telephones like the one in the photo above – nothing like today's cordless phones and cell phones.

For instance, we still say a phone is ringing, even though telephones haven't had bells for years. The round dials on phones also disappeared decades ago. But when we make calls, we still dial numbers – even though we actually enter them on a keypad or screen. Pressing a key is also the usual way to end a call on a cordless phone or cell phone. Although we still use "to hang up" which describes the action of putting the receiver back on a traditional telephone.

17.2 Reading

It's not just the English used to describe the operation of telephones that's confusing. Many of the English words and phrases used during phone conversations can also seem strange to non-native speakers. How much telephoning English do you know? Take the quiz below.

What do you say when …
1. you answer the phone and the caller asks to talk to you (e.g. "Can I speak to Alex, please?")?
2. you're busy and you'd like to phone the caller later?
3. the caller wants to speak to your colleague, and you connect the call to your colleague's phone?
4. you'd like to ask the caller to wait for a moment?
5. the caller wants to speak to your colleague, and your colleague is standing next to you?
6. the caller wants to speak to your colleague, but your colleague is currently on the phone?

Speaking.

I'll transfer you.

Please hold.

I'll put him/her on.

I'm afraid the line's busy.

Can I call you back?

17.3 Reading

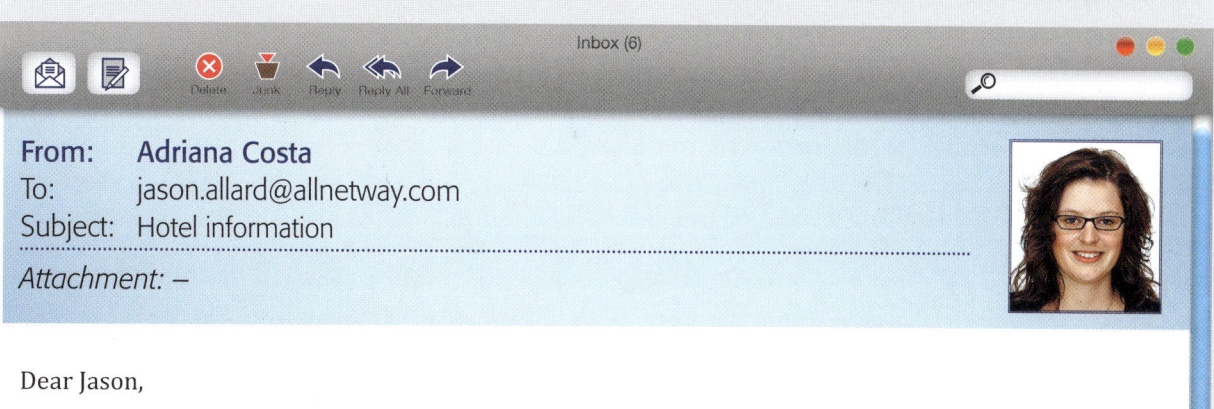

From: Adriana Costa
To: jason.allard@allnetway.com
Subject: Hotel information
Attachment: –

Dear Jason,

I hope you're well. I guess you're pretty busy with organizing the conference next month. On the subject of the conference, my boss Geraldine Marsa phoned me earlier. She asked if I could give her some information about the hotel. And there were a couple of questions I couldn't answer. There isn't much information on the website, and for some reason I can't get through to the hotel using the phone number given on the site. So maybe you can help?

She asked me if the hotel has a parking garage. Also, she wants to know whether it's possible to check in during the night. She's planning to drive there and will probably arrive late.

Best regards,

Adriana

17

17.1 Listening (Track 4)

Part A Try to think of five different words and phrases that mean `to telephone`. Use them to complete 1–5 below.

1 to _____ someone
2 to _____ someone
3 to _____ someone a _____
4 to _____ someone a _____
5 to _____ a _____ _____

Part B You're going to hear five extracts from conversations about telephoning. Listen and complete A–E. Then compare the words and phrases with those you wrote in Part A.

A I'll _____ you sometime next week.
B I'll _____ you later and give you the details.
C I just need to _____ a _____ .
D I'll _____ you a _____ as soon as I get home.
E I'll _____ you a _____ from the airport.

17.2 Listening (Track 5–6)

Part A You're going to hear five extracts from phone conversations. In each one, you'll hear a beep in place of a missing word or phrase. Each time, choose the word or phrase that's missing from A–E.

1	A Speaking.
2	B Please hold.
3	C I'll put him on.
4	D Can I call you back?
5	E The line's busy.

Part B Now listen to the complete extracts and check your answers to Part A.

17.3 Listening (Track 7)

Part A You're going to hear four questions about travel information which you probably won't be able to answer. However, imagine you know someone who can answer them. As you listen, write down key information from each question, so that you can use the notes to ask the other person.

1 _____
2 _____
3 _____
4 _____

Part B Imagine you're reporting the questions in Part A to the person you know. Complete the sentences below using your notes from 1–4.

1 *She asked*
2 *He asked*
3 *She wants to know*
4 *He asked me*

17.1 Follow-up

Complete 1–5, using words from the text in Reading 17.1.

1. a word to describe the sound a phone makes: _____
2. a word to describe putting a number into a phone: _____
3. words to describe ending a call: _____ _____
4. phones you can use anywhere outdoors: _____ _____
5. phones you can use anywhere inside a building: _____ _____

17.2 Follow-up

Choose suitable telephoning expressions to match 1–6 below. You could look at Reading 17.2 to help you.

1. Ask the caller to wait.

2. Ask the caller if you can phone him/her later.

3. Tell the caller you're connecting him/her to someone else's phone.

4. Tell the caller you're passing the phone to Ken, who's standing next to you.

5. The caller asks to speak to your colleague. Say your colleague is on the phone.

6. The caller asks to talk to you, not knowing you're the person on the phone. Reply.

17.3 Follow-up

Answer these questions about the email in Reading 17.3.

1. What job is Jason doing at the moment?

2. What general information did Adriana's boss ask for?

3. Why couldn't Adriana find the information she needed?

4. What specific questions did Adriana's boss ask?

American English	British English
cell phone	mobile phone

17

17.1 Language Summary — Talking about telephoning

I'll
- ▶ telephone you next week.
- ▶ phone
- ▶ call
- ▶ give you ▶ a call next week.
  - ▶ a ring

Excuse me. I need to make a phone call.
I'll be out, but if you need to, you can call me on my
- ▶ cell phone.
- ▶ mobile phone.
- ▶ mobile.

I thought I heard something. I thought my phone was ringing.
On this phone, to dial a number, you touch the numbers on the screen.

→ LANGUAGE PRACTICE 17.1 → PAGE 103

17.2 Language Summary — Getting through on the phone

Hello? – Hello, Sandra? – Yes, speaking.
I'm sorry, I'm busy at the moment. Can I call you back?
Can I speak to Eric, please? – Yes, just a moment.
Eric's standing next to me. I'll put him on.
Eric's in the other office. I'll transfer you.
One moment, please. Please hold.
I'm afraid Eric's on the phone. His line's busy.

→ LANGUAGE PRACTICE 17.2 → PAGE 104

17.3 Language Summary — Reporting information

What someone asked	Saying what the person asked
"Is the hotel near the station?"	He/She asked if/whether the hotel is/was near the station.
"Does the room have a safe?"	He/She asked if/whether the room has/had a safe.
"Where is the station?"	He/She asked where the station is/was.
"When does the store open?"	He/She asked when the store opens/opened.
"What time does it close?"	He/She asked what time it closes/closed.

→ LANGUAGE PRACTICE 17.3 → PAGE 104

Talking Point

Cell Phone Etiquette

1
There's no question that cell phones are extremely useful. But they can also be extremely annoying. Or, rather, people sometimes use them in annoying ways. As a result, in some countries a kind of "cell phone etiquette" is emerging – a list of do's and don'ts for using cell phones politely. But do people really agree on the basic social and professional rules for using cell phones? Or is "cell phone etiquette" still evolving?

2
Using the *Resource Sheet*, write a list of some examples of do's and don'ts for using cell phones politely, based on your own views.

3
Which do's and don'ts did you write down? Explain why you chose them.

4
Compare your list of do's and don'ts with those of other people in the group. Do you mostly agree or disagree on the points of "cell phone etiquette"?

UNIT 18
IN CONTROL

18.1 Talking about electrical devices
18.2 Understanding simple technical instructions
18.3 Describing controlling actions

18.1 Reading

MAKING SENSE OF COMPLEXITY, SIMPLICITY AND TECHNOLOGICAL PROGRESS

They say you can't stop progress. This fact is especially true with technology. But what does rapid technological progress mean for consumers? Are electrical devices getting more complicated to use? Or is more "intelligent" technology making life simpler for users?

Think about TVs as an example. Looking at the number of buttons on most remote controls, it seems modern television sets are much more complicated to use than old-fashioned ones. Old sets just had an on-off switch, a volume control and a few buttons for channels.

However, with old-fashioned TVs, tuning the set manually wasn't so simple, whereas today, "plug and play" technology allows you to just grab the power cable, put the plug in the socket and then let the software set up the TV automatically.

18.2 Reading

MT855 Tablet – Components and Controls

power adapter

Connect the power adapter to an electrical socket to recharge the battery. When the adapter is connected, the "charge" light will come on to show that the battery is charging. When the battery is fully charged, this light will go out. After charging the battery, always disconnect the power adapter from the socket.

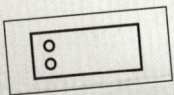
battery cover

Remove this cover to access the battery. When replacing the cover, push until the clip clicks into position.

battery

Before inserting or removing the battery, ensure the power adapter is disconnected.

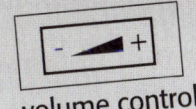
on-off switch

Press the button to turn on or turn off the device.

volume control

Press (+) to turn up the sound and (–) to turn down the sound.

18.3 Reading

Technical support – Q&A

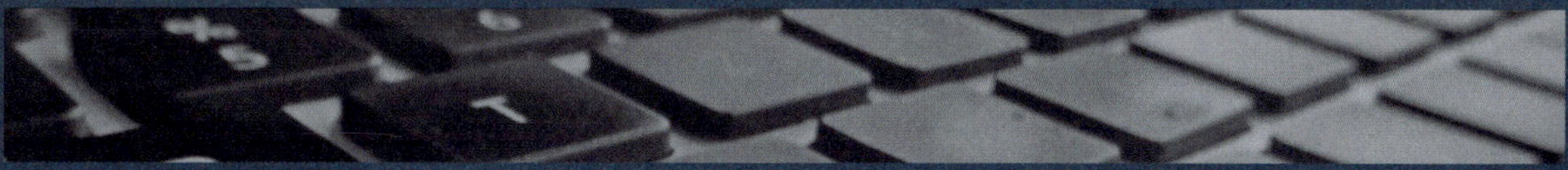

→ Question

The battery won't recharge on my tablet (MT855 model). When I plug the adapter in, the "charge" light comes on. But this doesn't charge the battery, even if I leave it for hours. When I unplug the adapter, the battery is always flat. It's impossible to turn the unit on without the adapter. However, when I take the battery cover off after trying to charge it, and touch the battery, it's always hot. So it seems that electricity is going through the battery while it's charging.

If the battery is dead, is it possible to buy a replacement? (The tablet is no longer under guarantee.) If it's not possible to replace the battery, and I just use the tablet with the power adapter, should I take the battery out?

18.1 Listening (Track 8)

You're going to hear Benjamin Leanne, an engineer, giving his views about complexity and simplicity on the subject of smartphones. Listen, then sum up what he says using the words and phrases from the interview, below.

1 functions
2 comparable
3 sophisticated, but simple

18.2 Listening (Track 9)

Use the words below to describe the actions in 1–5. Look at the diagrams to see the type of movement in the actions. Then listen and check your answers.

in   in   off   on   out

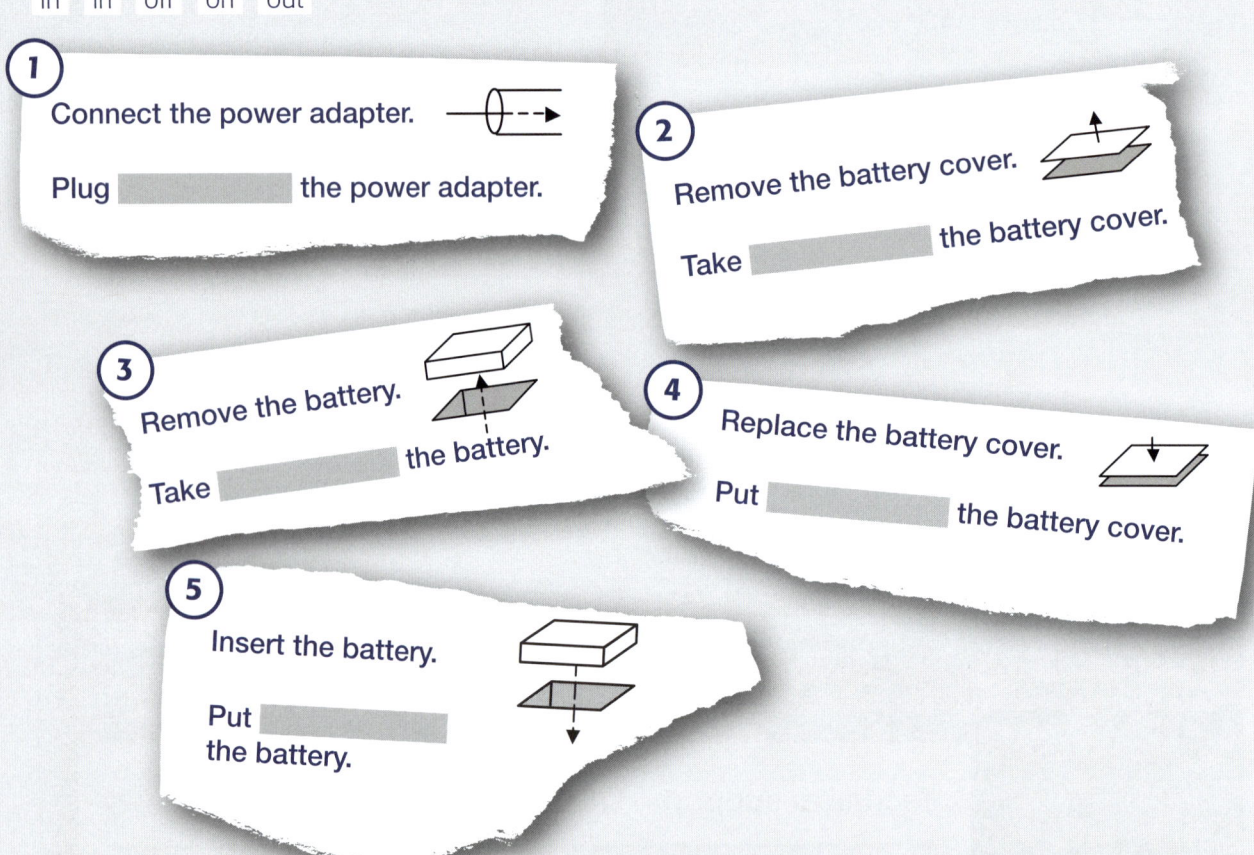

1 Connect the power adapter.
   Plug _____ the power adapter.

2 Remove the battery cover.
   Take _____ the battery cover.

3 Remove the battery.
   Take _____ the battery.

4 Replace the battery cover.
   Put _____ the battery cover.

5 Insert the battery.
   Put _____ the battery.

18.3 Listening (Track 10)

Complete the sentences about problems with a tablet computer. Use it and the words below. Then listen and check your answers.

in   on   out   out

1 The only way to make the tablet work is to plug it _____.
2 You have to leave the plug in. The power cuts off if you pull it _____.
3 If the tablet isn't plugged in, then you can't turn it _____.
4 I'm not sure if I should leave the battery in or take it _____.

18.1 Follow-up

Try to complete these extracts from the article in Reading 18.1. Then look at the article and check your answers.

1. Are electrical `d`_____ getting more complicated to use?
2. Looking at the number of `b`_____ on most remote `c`_____, it seems modern television sets are much more complicated to use than old-fashioned ones.
3. Old sets just had an `on-o`_____ `s`_____, a `v`_____ control and a few buttons for channels.
4. However, with old-fashioned TVs, tuning the set `m`_____ `lly` wasn't so simple …
5. … whereas today, "plug and play" technology allows you to just grab the power `c`_____, put the plug in the `s`_____ and then let the software set up the TV `a`_____ `lly`.

18.2 Follow-up

Answer these questions about the instructions for the tablet computer in Reading 18.2.

1. How do you recharge the battery of the tablet?
2. What shows that the battery is charging?
3. How do you know when the battery is charged?
4. To take out the battery, what do you have to do first?
5. What should you always do before taking out or putting in the battery?
6. What happens if you press "+"?

18.3 Follow-up

Move each highlighted word to a position later in the sentence. Then look at the text in Reading 18.3 and check your answers.

1. When I plug `in` the adapter, the "charge" light comes on.

2. It's impossible to turn `on` the unit without the adapter.

3. … when I take `off` the battery cover after trying to charge it …

4. … should I take `out` the battery?

18

18.1 Language Summary — Talking about electrical devices

To work, appliances such as TVs and washing machines use `electricity`.
TVs and washing machines are examples of `electrical appliances`.
Electrical appliances can be connected to electrical `sockets` in walls.
A `plug` is the part of an electrical appliance that you put into an electrical socket.
Plugs are connected to appliances by a long `cable/wire`.
Electrical appliances have an `on-off switch`, which you press to start or stop them.
Most TVs have a `remote control`, which allows you to control the TV from a distance.
TV remote controls generally have lots of `buttons` on them.
To control how loud the sound of a TV is, you use the `volume` control.
If you control something yourself (e.g. the volume of a TV), we say you do it `manually`.
If an appliance does something itself, we say it works `automatically`.

→ LANGUAGE PRACTICE 18.1 → PAGE 104

18.2 Language Summary — Understanding simple technical instructions

Press the on-off switch to `turn on` or `turn off` the appliance.
Use the volume control to `turn up` or `turn down` the sound.
Use the plug to `connect` the device to a socket. `Disconnect` the device after using it.
`Plug in` the device (= connect it). Then `unplug` it (= disconnect it).
When the device is connected, the light will `come on`. It will `go out` when disconnected.
There's no power left in the battery. You need to `charge/recharge` the battery.
First, `remove / take off` the battery cover so that the battery compartment is open.
Then `insert / put in` the battery.
Now that the battery is in the device, `replace / put back` the battery cover.

→ LANGUAGE PRACTICE 18.2 → PAGE 104

18.3 Language Summary — Describing controlling actions

Together	Split
`Plug in` the TV.	`Plug` the TV `in`.
`Turn on` the TV.	`Turn` the TV `on`.
`Turn up` the volume.	`Turn` the volume `up`.

`Plug` it `in`.	Not	Plug in it.
`Turn` it `on`.		Turn on it.

→ LANGUAGE PRACTICE 18.3 → PAGE 105

Talking Point

Lower-Voltage Lifestyle

1

The bestselling book *In Praise of Slow* makes a simple suggestion: that we should slow down. In today's fast-moving, wired world, perhaps that sounds like an obvious idea. However, the book reveals that our culture of speed is much deeper than we think, and its consequences are more negative than we realize. The author, journalist Carl Honoré, is not an anti-modernity fanatic. There are no extreme ideas about throwing away cell phones or adopting a hippy lifestyle. Instead, the book looks at how we can find a better balance, and how "finding our inner tortoise" can make us not just happier, but also more productive.

2

In your view, what are the different negative consequences of a fast pace of life? You could talk about the consequences on one or more of the following:
- personal health and happiness
- family life
- professional life

3

Talk about the possibility of living life at a slower pace:
- What aspects of life could you slow down?
- What would be the benefits?
- How easy/difficult would it be to slow down these aspects of life?

UNIT 19
SHELTER

19.1 Describing building interiors
19.2 Describing building exteriors
19.3 Describing designs

19.1 Reading

Finding a new place to live is tricky. To choose the right home successfully, you need the right strategy. First, that means you have to be realistic. Accept that you'll probably never find your ideal home, no matter how big your budget is. Then, make two decisions:

1 // Decide which aspects of your new home are most important to you, based on your lifestyle.

For example, is your top priority a spacious kitchen with an intelligent dishwasher, where you can cook passionately? Or do you just need a corner with a fridge, a microwave and a sink? Do you want a separate bath and shower? Or are bigger bedrooms with large closets more important than bathroom space?

2 // Decide if you want to do some work on the place and, if so, how much.

For many people, moving into a new home means new paint and wallpaper, and putting in your own drapes/curtains, carpets, etc. Of course, you can go much further than simply redecorating the living room. Deciding to do a big interior renovation – such as pulling out the kitchen or bathroom, and starting again – can offer some big advantages. But there are also disadvantages.

19.2 Reading

A GROWING TREND IN ARCHITECTURE
How plants are flourishing in building design

Traditionally, architects design buildings, and *landscape* architects design green spaces. However, the two jobs are moving closer together. Increasingly, plants are used, not just in gardens, but also to cover walls and roofs.

Why? One simple reason is, plants look nicer than many building materials. Concrete and steel look hard and cold, and even materials that are better-looking, such as bricks and stone, can appear ugly in large walls. So plants can be used to hide hard materials and give a softer, natural look.

One way to do this artificially is to use glass as a mirror for nature. Walls covered by reflective glass can be surrounded by trees, bushes, flowers and grass. This greenery is then reflected in the glass. But some architects are now covering their buildings, not with reflections of nature, but with the real thing. Two new words in architecture, with obvious meanings, are "greenwall" and "greenroof".

19.3 Reading

A: There's nothing wrong with bright colors in modern architecture, provided they're chosen carefully. In this case, that hasn't happened. The building may be original, but it's also ugly. The mix of colors looks old-fashioned, reminding you of the 1970s.

B: In my opinion, there's a golden rule in architecture: simple is beautiful. I think the facade of this building follows that rule. I know people always say that concrete is dull. Here, though, the very light gray doesn't give you that impression at all.

19.1 Listening (Track 11–12)

Part A You're going to hear Astrid Meacham, an architect, talking about the advantages and disadvantages of renovating home interiors. Listen, then answer the questions below about her opinions.

1. What's the main advantage of doing an interior renovation?
2. What word sums up the main disadvantage?
3. Which two rooms are the worst to renovate? Why?

Part B In Part A, the interviewer asks:
"Are renovations worth the money?"
Discuss this question. What's your opinion?

Part C Now listen to Astrid Meacham giving her views on the question above. Sum up the points she makes using the highlighted words from the interview, below. Compare Astrid's views with the opinions you gave in Part B.

a bad state   builders   underestimate

19.2 Listening (Track 13)

Part A Concrete, glass, bricks, stone, wood, etc. Materials give buildings their looks. But how should an architect choose what "material look" to give a building? Discuss your opinions on this question.

Part B Now listen to architect Astrid Meacham discussing the question from Part A. Sum up the reasons she gives for choosing materials. Compare them with the points you discussed in Part A.

19.3 Listening (Track 14)

You're going to hear a tour guide talking about the design of the stone columns on a building. She uses three words that are opposites of those below. Listen and write down the words to complete 1–3.

	Opposite
1 simple	
2 original	
3 light	

19.1 Follow-up

Look at the article in Reading 19.1. Find words in the text to match the descriptions below.

1 a type of oven that heats up food very quickly
2 a place to keep food cool
3 a machine that cleans plates, cups, etc. automatically
4 a liquid you put on with a brush to color a surface
5 a textile decoration for windows
6 places to keep clothing
7 soft coverings for floors

19.2 Follow-up

Answer these questions about the article in Reading 19.2.

1 What do landscape architects do?
2 Why are the jobs of landscape architect and architect moving closer together?
3 What's the problem with concrete and steel in building design?
4 What's the advantage of using plants in building design?
5 How can glass be used to give buildings a natural look?
6 Which new words in architecture describe the use of plants to cover buildings?

19.3 Follow-up

Look at the descriptions below. Which text in Reading 19.3 does each one describe? Write A or B.

1 The building isn't colorful.
2 The building doesn't look complicated.
3 The building doesn't look like other buildings.
4 The building doesn't look very modern.

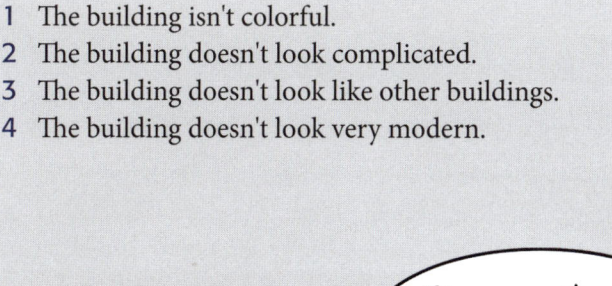

American English	British English
closet	wardrobe

19

19.1 Language Summary — Describing building interiors

You can change the color of a door by putting different-colored paint on it.
Paper that covers walls, to decorate them, is called wallpaper.
Curtains/Drapes are used to cover and decorate the insides of windows.
Soft material used to cover a floor is called a carpet.
In a kitchen, the hot and cold taps/faucets are found on the sink.
In a kitchen, the worktops are the surfaces where food is prepared.

Appliances that are often found in kitchens are:
- a dishwasher (for washing plates, glasses, etc. automatically)
- a refrigerator – or fridge, for short (for keeping food cool)
- an oven (for heating food)
- a microwave oven – or microwave, for short (for heating food very quickly)

→ LANGUAGE PRACTICE 19.1 → PAGE 105

19.2 Language Summary — Describing building exteriors

The walls of buildings are often built from bricks, which are small blocks made of clay.
When pieces of rock are used to build a wall, we say the wall is built from stone.
Concrete is a very common building material made from cement, sand and gravel.
Wood is a natural building material that we get from trees.
Glass is used in windows because you can see through it.
The roof – the top part of a building – must stop rain from getting into the building.
In gardens and the areas around buildings, you find different kinds of plants, such as flowers, bushes and, of course, grass, which covers lawns.

→ LANGUAGE PRACTICE 19.2 → PAGE 105

19.3 Language Summary — Describing designs

The main colors in the design are yellow and orange, so it looks very bright.
The only color in the design is gray, so it looks quite dull.
The color is a very dark brown – it's almost black.
The color is a very light yellow – it's almost white.
You can see that it's a new design. It looks really modern.
It looks like a design from 20 years ago. It's old-fashioned.
We've never seen anything like it before. It's certainly original.
How can anyone say it's beautiful? I think it looks horrible. It's ugly.

→ LANGUAGE PRACTICE 19.3 → PAGE 105

Talking Point

Defining "Palace"

1
The English word "palace" comes from *Palatium* – the Latin name for the Palatine Hill in Rome, where the emperor lived. Today, "palace" can mean the residence of a president or king or queen. Or, more generally, it means an exceptionally large, luxurious house – a dream home.

For some people, "dream home" and "exceptionally large, luxurious house" are the same thing. For others – no matter how big their budget – the ideal home would look nothing like the common image of a palace. It might be a small, cozy apartment. Or a rustic farmhouse. The definition of "palace" is a very personal thing.

2
Imagine you could afford to buy and maintain an exceptionally large, luxurious home. Decide if you would or wouldn't like to live in such a house, and explain why or why not. Or you may be undecided and could discuss things you'd like and things you'd dislike.

3
Imagine you could afford to buy more or less any home you wanted. With money no object, what would your dream home be like? Talk about:
- the location of the home
- the size of the building and surrounding land
- types and numbers of rooms, and special features (e.g. swimming pool, sauna)
- the style of the building and the interior

UNIT 20
HARD WORK

20.1 Discussing everyday tasks
20.2 Describing and comparing actions
20.3 Describing past routines

20.1 Reading

To do
Vacuum bedrooms
Clean upstairs windows
Wash and iron laundry
Cut grass
Sweep patio

To do
Pay electricity bill
File bills and clean up desk
Sort out insurance
Put away books
Throw out old newspapers

20.2 Reading

No matter how simple a job seems, there are always a few tricks of the trade. Check out these tips from professionals on two of the most common household tasks.

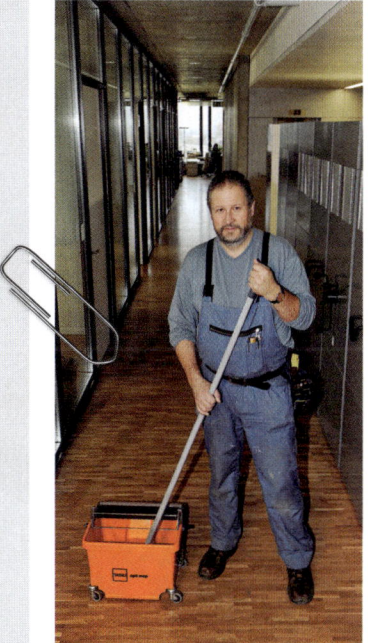

Sam Adair
Cleaner
30 years' experience

"When you wash a floor, always use very hot water. You need heat to clean things well. Hot water also dries fast. And, while you're washing the floor, change the water regularly. It's surprising how quickly it gets dirty. Obviously, you can't clean things properly using dirty water."

Helene Giraud
Chef
18 years' experience

"When you're cutting food in the kitchen, in order to work safely, always use a sharp knife. That might sound strange. But sharp knives cut easily, so you don't have to press them down hard. If you're only pressing on the knife gently, you can work carefully, so there's less chance you'll slip and cut yourself."

20.3 Reading

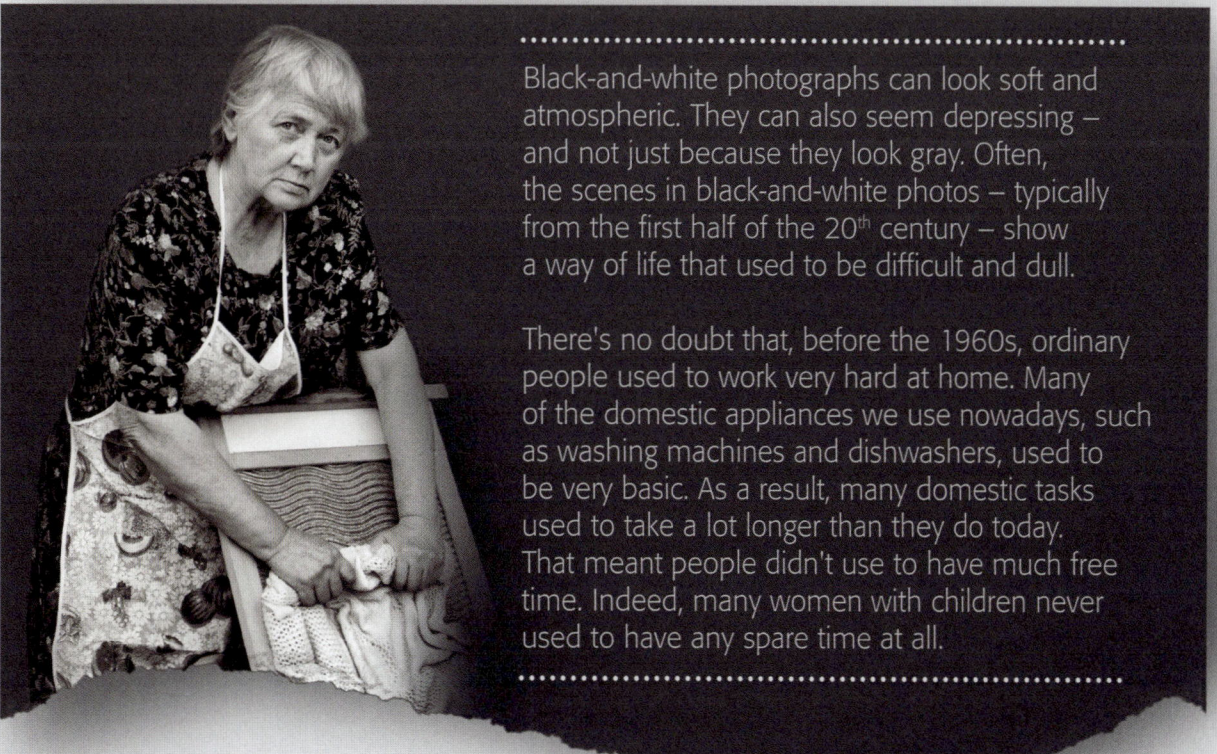

Black-and-white photographs can look soft and atmospheric. They can also seem depressing – and not just because they look gray. Often, the scenes in black-and-white photos – typically from the first half of the 20th century – show a way of life that used to be difficult and dull.

There's no doubt that, before the 1960s, ordinary people used to work very hard at home. Many of the domestic appliances we use nowadays, such as washing machines and dishwashers, used to be very basic. As a result, many domestic tasks used to take a lot longer than they do today. That meant people didn't use to have much free time. Indeed, many women with children never used to have any spare time at all.

20.1 Listening (Track 15)

Part A Use the words below to complete the interview about paperwork. Then listen and check your answers.

`away` `file` `out` `out` `put` `sort` `throw`

I'm not one of these people who always pay their bills at the last minute. I hate admin, so I prefer to 1 _SORT_ 2 _OUT_ payments and things like that immediately, to get them out of the way. As soon as I've paid bills, I 3 _FILE_ them in boxes and 4 _PUT_ them 5 _AWAY_ in a closet, out of sight. And, if there are any papers I don't need, I just 6 _THROW_ them 7 _OUT_. I hate to see paperwork lying around.

Part B Compare your views about administration and paperwork with those discussed in the interview above.

20.2 Listening (Track 16)

Part A You're going to hear Tom Clayton, a builder with over 20 years' experience, giving some tips on how to use simple digging tools. Before listening, try to complete the transcript below.

When you're doing a very physical job, such as digging with a spade, working 1 _harder_ (+ hard) doesn't mean digging 2 _FASTER_ (+ fast). Don't dig like crazy and tire yourself out in an hour. If you work 3 _LESS QUICKLY_ (– quick), you'll do more in a day.

And when you dig with a pickaxe, never lift it higher than your shoulders. Pickaxes work 4 _better_ (+ good) and are much less tiring to work with when you swing them 5 _less AGRESSIVELY_ (– aggressive) and use them 6 _more CAREFULLY_ (+ careful). By keeping the tool low, you'll also work a lot 7 _more SAFELY_ (+ safe).

Part B Now listen and check your answers.

20.3 Listening (Track 17)

Part A You're going to hear Ellie Amundsen discussing what it used to be like washing laundry in the 1960s. Listen, then explain why the job was much harder, compared with today.

Part B Now <u>underline</u> `could` or `couldn't` to complete these extracts from the interview. Then listen again and check your answers.

1 I had a washing machine, so I `could/couldn't` wash my laundry with that.
2 You `could/couldn't` just put the laundry in, turn it on and leave it.
3 Then you `could/couldn't` start it up immediately – the water took time to heat up.
4 And then you `could/couldn't` leave it to wash everything – that part was automatic.
5 The old machine `could/couldn't` spin the water out like modern ones can.

20.1 Follow-up

Match the pairs to complete the "to do" list. Then look at Reading 20.1 and check your answers.

Vacuum	1	8	A	desk
Wash and iron	2	4	B	patio
Cut	3	1	C	bedrooms
Sweep	4	6	D	old newspapers
Pay	5	2	E	laundry
Throw out	6	3	F	grass
Put away	7	7	G	books
Clean up	8	5	H	electricity bill

20.2 Follow-up

Look at the tips in 1–7. Use the correct forms of the words below to complete them.

careful   easy   fast   gentle   good   hard   regular

1 Hot water dries FAST .
2 Change the water REGULARLY .
3 You need heat to clean things WELL .
4 Sharp knives cut EASILY .
5 If a knife is sharp, you don't have to press it down HARD .
6 With a sharp knife, you only need to press it GENTLY .
7 A sharp knife allows you to work more CAREFULLY .

20.3 Follow-up

Answer these questions about the article in Reading 20.3.

1 According to the article, what lifestyle do black-and-white photos often show?

2 What did home life use to be like for ordinary people before the 1960s?

3 What did domestic appliances use to be like?

4 What does the article say about leisure?

5 What does it say about women?

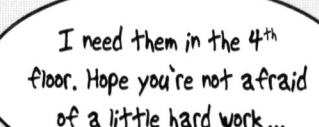

I need them in the 4th floor. Hope you're not afraid of a little hard work...

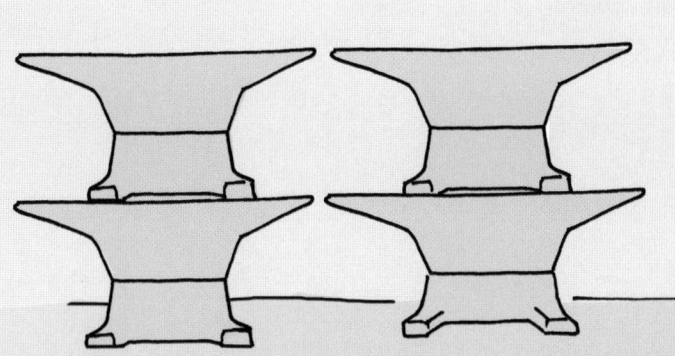

20.1 Language Summary — Discussing everyday tasks

The floor's dirty. I need to clean it.
To clean some things, you can use water to wash them.
A vacuum cleaner is an electrical appliance often used to clean floors. For example, you can use it to vacuum a carpet.
After you've washed clothes, when they're dry, you can smooth them using an appliance called an iron, which gets very hot. This is used to iron the clothes.
You need to cut the grass / mow the lawn regularly, using a lawnmower.
A brush used to sweep a floor is called a broom.
The house is a mess. We need to clean up.
We can put away all these things. They can go in the cupboard.
Let's throw away all this stuff. It's all garbage.
I've got some things to organize. There are a few things I need to sort out.

→ LANGUAGE PRACTICE 20.1 → PAGE 106

20.2 Language Summary — Describing and comparing actions

Most words for describing actions end in –ly.
He's a quick worker.   He works quickly.
That looks safe.   You're working safely.

Common exceptions:
He's a fast worker.   He works fast.   No change
He's a hard worker.   He works hard.   No change
He's a good worker.   He works well.   Irregular

To make comparisons:
He works more safely. / He works less safely.
He works faster.
He works harder.
He works better.

→ LANGUAGE PRACTICE 20.2 → PAGE 106

20.3 Language Summary — Describing past routines

One hundred years ago, most people
- used to work long hours.
- didn't use to have much spare time.
- never used to go on vacation.
- could only afford to buy basic things.
- couldn't afford to go on vacation.

→ LANGUAGE PRACTICE 20.3 → PAGE 106

Talking Point

Working Life in Black-and-White

1
Smith, Baker, Mason, Fisher, Glover, Thatcher, Miller, Cooper, Carter, Shepherd: Some of the most common surnames in English-speaking countries originate from job titles. The same tradition exists in many other languages, too. Family names offer interesting insights into working life in the past.

Do you know or can you guess which jobs – past and present – are described by the ten surnames above? Discuss your ideas, then compare them with the answers on the *Resource Sheet*.

2
Talk about any surnames in your language/country that refer to jobs from the past and present.

3
Talk about a job that existed many years ago, which you know something about. It may be a job that no longer exists or a job that still exists today but used to be very different in the past (e.g. farming). You could talk about a job that a member of your family – such as one of your grandparents or great-grandparents – used to do.

Grammar Summary 16–20

Reported speech

Use reported speech to say what somebody said. Change statements in the following way:

"I live in Madrid."	She said she lives in Madrid.
	or She said she lived in Madrid.
"I'll visit again soon."	She said she'll visit again soon.
	or She said she would visit again soon.
"I can come to the meeting."	She said she can come to the meeting.
	or She said she could come to the meeting.

When you are reporting what somebody asked, change the word order in the following way:

"Where is the station?"	She asked (me) where the station is/was.
"What sort of car do you have?"	She wanted to know what sort of car I have/had.

When you are reporting closed questions, change the word order and use if or whether.

"Is the airport far from town?"	She asked if / whether the airport is/was far from town.
"Will the show be on again?"	She asked if / whether the show will/would be on again.

Adverbs of manner

Use adverbs of manner with verbs to describe actions in more detail. Put the adverb after the verb.
He's running slowly. She drives carefully. Work safely.

	Adjective	Adverb
Most adverbs of manner are adjectives + –ly.	slow	slowly
	quick	quickly
	safe	safely
	careful	carefully
Some adverbs of manner don't take –ly.	fast	fast
	hard	hard
	good	well

Make comparisons with adverbs of manner in the following way:
with adverbs ending in –ly, use more or less.   ▶ I work more quickly than he does.
with fast and hard, add –er.   ▶ I can run faster than he can.
with well, use better.   ▶ I can drive better than he can.

Grammar Summary 16–20

Two-word verbs

Some verbs are used with a second word, such as in , out , on , off . Sometimes, the second word describes movement or position. For example:

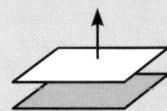
Take off the cover.

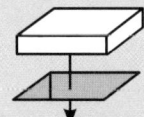
Put in the battery.

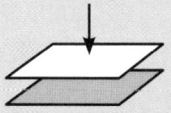
Put on the cover.

Sometimes, the second word does not describe movement or position. For example: clean up (= clean), sort out (= organize). Verbs like these are called phrasal verbs.

When a sentence has an object, the object can usually be placed between the two parts of the verb. This is common in informal, spoken English.
- Take off the cover.
- Put in the batteries.
- Clean up the mess.
- Sort out the problem.
- Take the cover off .
- Put the batteries in .
- Clean the mess up .
- Sort the problem out .

When an object is replaced by a pronoun, such as it or them , the pronoun must usually be placed between the two parts of the verb.

Take off the cover. / Take the cover off .   Take it off .   Not   Take off it.
Put in the batteries. / Put the batteries in .   Put them in .   Put in them.

Past situations with *used to*

Use used to to talk about past situations that lasted quite a long time and that are now finished.
I used to live in that town.
(I lived in the town for a period of time, but I don't live there any more.)

In negative sentences, use didn't use to or never used to .
I didn't use to eat tomatoes when I was a child.
I never used to eat tomatoes when I was a child.

32

Vocabulary Summary 16–20

Telephoning

to phone	cell/mobile phone	to hang up	I'll put him/her on.
to call	cordless phone	Speaking.	Please hold.
to make a phone call	the phone's ringing	I'll call you back.	The line's busy.
to give (you) a call	to dial a number	I'll transfer you.	

Appliances

device	on-off switch	automatic	to replace
gadget	volume control	manual	to insert
appliance	power cable	to connect	to turn on
wire	plug	to disconnect	to turn off
cable	to plug in	to charge	to turn up
button	to unplug	to recharge	to turn down
remote control	socket	to remove	

Building interiors

dishwasher	sink/basin	closet/wardrobe	drapes/curtains
refrigerator/fridge	bathtub	paint	carpet
microwave (oven)	shower	wallpaper	

Building exteriors

wall	brick	plant	flower
roof	stone	garden	grass
concrete	wood	tree	lawn
steel	glass	bush	

Designs

light	dull	beautiful	traditional
dark	modern	ugly	simple
bright	old-fashioned	original	complex

Everyday tasks

to vacuum	to iron	broom	to put away
vacuum cleaner	to cut the grass	to pay	to throw out
to clean	to mow the lawn	to file	
to wash	lawnmower	to clean up	
iron	to sweep	to sort out	

Skills Summary 16–20

After Units 16 to 20, you can ...

Skill	Section
▶ express opinions	16.1
▶ link ideas	16.1
▶ express degrees of agreement	16.2
▶ express degrees of disagreement	16.2
▶ report comments people made	16.3
▶ report views people expressed	16.3
▶ refer to telephoning actions	17.1
▶ answer the phone	17.2
▶ deal with incoming calls	17.2
▶ ask to speak to people on the phone	17.2
▶ report information	17.3
▶ refer to parts of appliances	18.1
▶ understand technical instructions for common devices	18.2
▶ describe physical actions for using appliances	18.3
▶ describe household fittings and furnishings	19.1
▶ describe external features of buildings	19.2
▶ refer to common materials	19.2
▶ refer to common plants	19.2
▶ describe styles and colors	19.3
▶ refer to everyday work tasks	20.1
▶ describe physical actions	20.2
▶ compare physical actions	20.2
▶ describe routines in the past	20.3
▶ say what was/wasn't possible in the past	20.3

UNIT 21
PROBLEMS

21.1 Discussing problems and difficulties
21.2 Making and responding to suggestions
21.3 Discussing past problems and solutions

21.1 Reading

From: Angela Roberts
To: john.carter@allnetway.com
Subject: Delay
Attachment: –

The latest news is, I'm still stuck at the airport. It's still snowing, and the runway's still closed. And the problem is, there's still no news about the length of the delay. In other words, nothing has changed since my last message. But I'm emailing you anyway. I've got nothing else to do!

The trouble is we're not getting much information from the airline. So it's difficult to know if the runway is going to open at all today. That means, it's hard to decide what to do. If somebody could confirm that no planes will be able to take off, then I could go home and come back tomorrow.
But I can't do that unless it's certain that we won't be able to fly. I can understand that it's impossible to know exactly how long it'll take to clear the runway. But surely they have a rough idea. Especially looking at how hard it's snowing now. It seems pretty obvious that things are getting worse, not better.

Anyway, as soon as I find out what's happening, I'll let you know.

21.2 Reading

We welcome your suggestions on how we could improve the services we provide at this airport. Please write your suggestion below and put this form in the Suggestions Box. Thank you.

SUGGESTION

What about having a large screen in the departures area that can show more detailed information about delays and problems with flights? The departures screen shows very short messages, like "Delayed". But there's only enough space on it for one or two words. So why don't you have a separate screen that's big enough to give more detailed information, such as the reason for the delay?

As a passenger, I find it very frustrating when a flight is delayed, and I don't know why or for how long. How about solving this problem by having better information screens? And you could use them to show ads when there are no problems to report.

21.3 Reading

Flying is the best way to get to places fast. It's also the best way to arrive late. Bad weather, technical problems, air traffic congestion and strikes are all common causes of flight delays. But on April 14, 2010, air travel in Europe was hit by an unusual problem: a cloud of ash from Eyjafjallajökull, a volcano in Iceland. The disruption caused by the unpronounceable volcano was unprecedented. The week after, about 100,000 European flights were canceled. And an incident 28 years earlier provides scary proof of why ash clouds are such a serious problem for jet aircraft.

On June 24, 1982, British Airways Flight 9 from London to Auckland flew into a volcanic ash cloud 37,000 feet above Indonesia. The cloud wasn't visible on the plane's weather radar, so the pilots weren't able to avoid it. Within a few minutes, all four of the Boeing 747's engines stopped. Immediately, the pilots tried to start the engines, but they didn't manage to get them going. They then calculated that it was possible for the plane to stay in the air, descending gently without power, for 23 minutes.

Eventually, at an altitude of about 13,000 feet, the pilots managed to start one engine. Soon after, they were able to start another. Finally, the plane's four engines were running again, and the pilots managed to land the aircraft safely at Jakarta Airport.

21.1 Listening (Track 18)

Look at the pairs of sentences about travel problems below. Complete the second sentences using different words and phrases that mean the same as those in the first sentences. Then listen and check your answers.

1. It's hard to find your way around the airport.
   It's _____ to find your way around the airport.

2. It won't be possible for us to get there on time.
   We won't _____ _____ _____ get there on time.

3. It's not possible to get a refund with this type of ticket.
   It's _____ to get a refund with this type of ticket.

4. The problem is, if you buy a ticket for immediate travel, it's really expensive.
   The _____ is, if you buy a ticket for immediate travel, it's really expensive.

5. I don't think it will be possible for you to get a seat on the flight.
   I don't think you will _____ _____ _____ get a seat on the flight.

21.2 Listening (Track 19–21)

Part A Listen to five suggestions about travel plans. As you listen, make notes below. After hearing each one, sum up what the suggestion is about. Also say what phrase is used to start each suggestion.

1.
2.
3.
4.
5.

Part B Listen to the suggestions again, and – this time – to the other person's reply. Does the other person agree (A) or disagree (D) with each suggestion?

1. A D
2. A D
3. A D
4. A D
5. A D

Part C Listen to the first parts of the replies again. Write down the phrases.

1. _____ _____ .
2. _____ _____ _____ _____ to walk?
3. _____ _____ _____ .
4. _____ , _____ _____ .
5. _____ _____ ?

21.3 Listening (Track 22)

Listen to the extracts from the article about ash clouds. Underline the letter that's silent (not pronounced) in the highlighted words.

1. … they didn't manage to get them going.
2. … the pilots managed to start one engine.

21.1 Follow-up

Answer these questions about the email in Reading 21.1.

1 Why are flights delayed?

2 Why does the writer criticize the airline?

3 What does she plan to do if the runway doesn't open today?

4 Why can't she go ahead with her plan for the moment?

5 What does she think will happen, and why?

21.2 Follow-up

Fill in the missing words and underline the correct words to complete the suggestions below. Then compare your answers with the form in Reading 21.2.

1 What _____ have/having a large screen in the departures area?
2 Why _____ you have/having a screen that gives detailed information?
3 How _____ solve/solving this problem by having better screens?
4 You _____ use/using them to show ads when there are no problems.

21.3 Follow-up

Look the article in Reading 21.3. Are the sentences below true or false?

1 The pilots of BA Flight 9 saw the ash cloud on the radar.   T   F
2 After flying into the ash, all the plane's engines stopped.   T   F
3 The pilots were able to start the engines immediately.   T   F
4 The pilots managed to fly the plane for a time without power.   T   F
5 Eventually, the pilots managed to start all the plane's engines. T   F
6 After the incident, the plane was able to land normally.   T   F

"Take your time. We still have 10 minutes before take off."

38

21

21.1 Language Summary — Discussing problems and difficulties

| The problem is , | flights often get delayed. |
| The trouble is , | the weather's often bad here. |

It's difficult to	know what time I'll arrive.
It's hard to	predict what's going to happen.
It's impossible to	

| I ▸ can | get a flight today . | I ▸ will be able to | get a flight tomorrow . |
| ▸ can't | | ▸ won't be able to | |

→ LANGUAGE PRACTICE 21.1 → PAGE 106

21.2 Language Summary — Making and responding to suggestions

| Shall we | take a break? |
| Why don't we | |

| Let's | take a break. |
| We could | |

| How about | taking a break? |
| What about | |

- ▸ Good idea.
- ▸ That sounds good.
- ▸ Why not?

→ LANGUAGE PRACTICE 21.2 → PAGE 107

21.3 Language Summary — Discussing past problems and solutions

Now	In the past	
I can do it.	I ▸ was able to ▸ managed to	do it.
I can't do it.	I ▸ wasn't able to ▸ didn't manage to	do it.

→ LANGUAGE PRACTICE 21.3 → PAGE 107

Talking Point 21

Blue-Sky Thinking

1
The cargo plane you were flying has just made an emergency landing. Fortunately, you and your copilot are unhurt. Unfortunately, you're in the middle of the desert. What's more, the plane's radio and navigation equipment have failed. That's why you got lost on your way to the gold mine, to which you were carrying food and supplies, and why you used up all your fuel and had to land.

There's nothing but sand as far as the eye can see, although you can't actually see very far through the heat haze. It's incredibly hot, even in the shade of the aircraft wing where you're now sitting. Already, you're drinking out of one of the 360 bottles of mineral water from the cargo hold.

2
With a partner, find information in text **1** that will help you decide what to do in this situation. Make notes, then sum up the information you wrote down. Say why you think the information is important.

3
Spend a few minutes doing some "blue-sky thinking" about different things you could do to get out of this situation. In other words, suggest as many possibilities as you can – but don't discuss the pros and cons of your ideas for the moment. Make a note of your ideas so that you can sum them up.

4
Compare your ideas with the suggestions on the *Resource Sheet*. Discuss the pros and cons of the ideas. Then make a decision on what to do. Be prepared to explain why you made your decision.

UNIT 22
PEOPLE AND PLACES

22.1 Discussing social issues
22.2 Referring to places, people and things
22.3 Discussing city attractions

22.1 Reading

WHERE'S THE BEST PLACE IN THE WORLD TO LIVE?

The above question sounds pretty subjective. However, it is possible to find an objective answer.

Every year, the consulting firm Mercer publishes a detailed *Quality of Living Survey*, which evaluates over 200 cities around the world. It then ranks them from best to worst.

The survey analyzes a number of issues. These include: education, health, crime, real estate, public transportation, the economy, the climate, pollution, recreation and food. One of the main objectives of the survey is to provide information to international companies who send their people to live and work abroad.

22.2 Reading

BEEN THERE? IMPRESSED? DISAPPOINTED? HAVE YOUR SAY.

★☆☆☆☆
I went in early spring and it was dead. There wasn't anything to do at all. I couldn't find any restaurants that were open. There was nowhere to go even if you just wanted a drink. Every meal or drink I had was at the hotel – I had no choice. Don't go out of season. It's like a ghost town.

★★★★☆
We never got bored while we were there in summer. There was always something to do or somewhere to go and visit. And it was good value for money. In two weeks, we spent almost nothing.

★★★★★
I found the people were very nice. Everybody was friendly. If you met somebody, they always gave you a smile and said hello. As a tourist, you felt really well looked after. The locals did everything they could to make you feel welcome. We didn't meet anybody who was unpleasant.

★☆☆☆☆
I got the impression that nobody was interested in us – they just wanted our money. I've seen some tacky places before, but I haven't seen anywhere as commercialized as that. In every street you walked down, there were just gift stores everywhere. It's just a tourist trap.

22.3 Reading

WHY MARKETERS ARE INVENTING CAPITAL CITIES

Cities are always looking for new ways to sell themselves. Sometimes, their objective is to bring in tourists. Sometimes, it's to attract new residents or businesses.

Fill in the blanks

How do you sell a city? One of the current buzzwords in city marketing is "capital". By describing a place as "the capital of (something)" – such as nightlife or business – you suggest that it's the best at something.

For example, you could call a city "The art capital of the United States", "The gastronomic capital of India" or "The business capital of Europe". Depending on a city's credentials and boastfulness, it can sell itself as a big capital ("The cultural capital of Asia") or a smaller one ("The music capital of the Southwest"). The idea is to say what's unique about the place – what marketers call a Unique Selling Point (USP).

22

22.1 Listening (Track 23)

Part A You're going to hear four extracts from an interview with a woman. She's going to give her opinions about different social issues. Listen and match each extract to one of the issues in A–D.

1   A   crime
2   B   health
3   C   real estate
4   D   the economy

Part B Listen again. For each extract, write down some key words and phrases from the interview that allowed you to identify the issue being discussed.

1
2
3
4

22.2 Listening (Track 24)

Complete the conversation below with `anywhere`, `everywhere`, `nowhere` or `somewhere`. You will need to use some words more than once. Then listen and check your answers.

anywhere   everywhere   nowhere   somewhere

A: Is there **1** _____ near here where I can get something to eat? I've been walking around for ages. I've looked **2** _____ .
B: I'm afraid there's **3** _____ to get food here. You'd have to go into town. What sort of place are you looking for? A restaurant? A snack bar?
A: It doesn't matter. **4** _____ , really. The nearest place there is.
B: There's **5** _____ just next to the train station where you can get sandwiches. I think that's the nearest place from here. I don't know **6** _____ closer than that.

22.3 Listening (Track 25)

Part A You're going to hear three extracts from conversations about things to do in cities. Listen and match the extracts to the topics in A–C.

1   A   food and drink
2   B   shows and entertainment
3   C   history and culture

Part B Listen again. For each extract, write down some key words from the conversation that helped you to identify the topic.

1
2
3

22.1 Follow-up

Look at the second paragraph of the article in Reading 22.1. Find issues in the text to match the examples below. The first one is done for you.

Issue	Example	Issue	Example
1 food	restaurants	5	typical weather
2	employment	6	buses and trains
3	sports facilities	7	schools and colleges
4	poor air quality	8	houses and apartments

22.2 Follow-up

Complete 1–8 using the words below. Then look at Reading 22.2 and check your answers.

anybody   anything   anywhere   somebody   something   somewhere   nobody   nothing   nowhere

1 I went in early spring and it was dead. There wasn't _____ to do at all.
2 There was _____ to go even if you just wanted a drink.
3 There was always _____ to do or _____ to go and visit.
4 In two weeks, we spent almost _____.
5 If you met _____, they always gave you a smile and said hello.
6 We didn't meet _____ who was unpleasant.
7 I got the impression that _____ was interested in us.
8 I've seen some tacky places before, but I haven't seen _____ as commercialized as that.

22.3 Follow-up

Answer these questions about the article in Reading 22.3.

1 What are two reasons why cities market themselves?

2 If a city is marketed as the capital of something, what does this say about the city?

3 Which capital city in the article relates to food?

4 What does "USP" stand for, and what does it mean?

22.1 Language Summary — Discussing social issues

Issue	Examples
Education	Who should pay for students to go to college?
	Should the government spend more on schools?
Health	How long do patients have to wait to get medical care?
	Are hospitals recruiting enough doctors and nurses?
	Is the cost of drugs too high?
Crime	Should there be more jails for the growing number of prisoners?
	Would it be better to increase the number of police officers?
The economy	Too many people are out of work. How can we reduce unemployment?
	Is the economy slowing? What's the risk of a recession?
	Can people afford to buy homes? Are real-estate prices too high?

→ LANGUAGE PRACTICE 22.1 → PAGE 107

22.2 Language Summary — Referring to places, people and things

Things: A plane is something that you can fly.
Places: An airport is somewhere that planes can fly to and from.
People: A pilot is somebody / someone who flies a plane.

Questions: Is there anything/ anybody/ anywhere … ?
Positive: There's something/ somebody/ somewhere …
Negative: There's nothing/ nobody/ nowhere …
There isn't anything/ anybody/ anywhere …

→ LANGUAGE PRACTICE 22.2 → PAGE 107

22.3 Language Summary — Discussing city attractions

A visit to the museum offers a view of life in the past.
Visitors to the art gallery can see over 500 paintings.
In the center of the park, there's a stone statue of the country's first president.
Currently, there are four different shows to see at the theater.
For those who enjoy live music, there'll be several big concerts in town this summer.
The stadium can hold 40,000 people at sporting events and concerts.
Is there anywhere we can go to sit down and have a drink? A cafe or a bar?
You can buy hot meals there, to eat at home. It's a takeout.

→ LANGUAGE PRACTICE 22.3 → PAGE 108

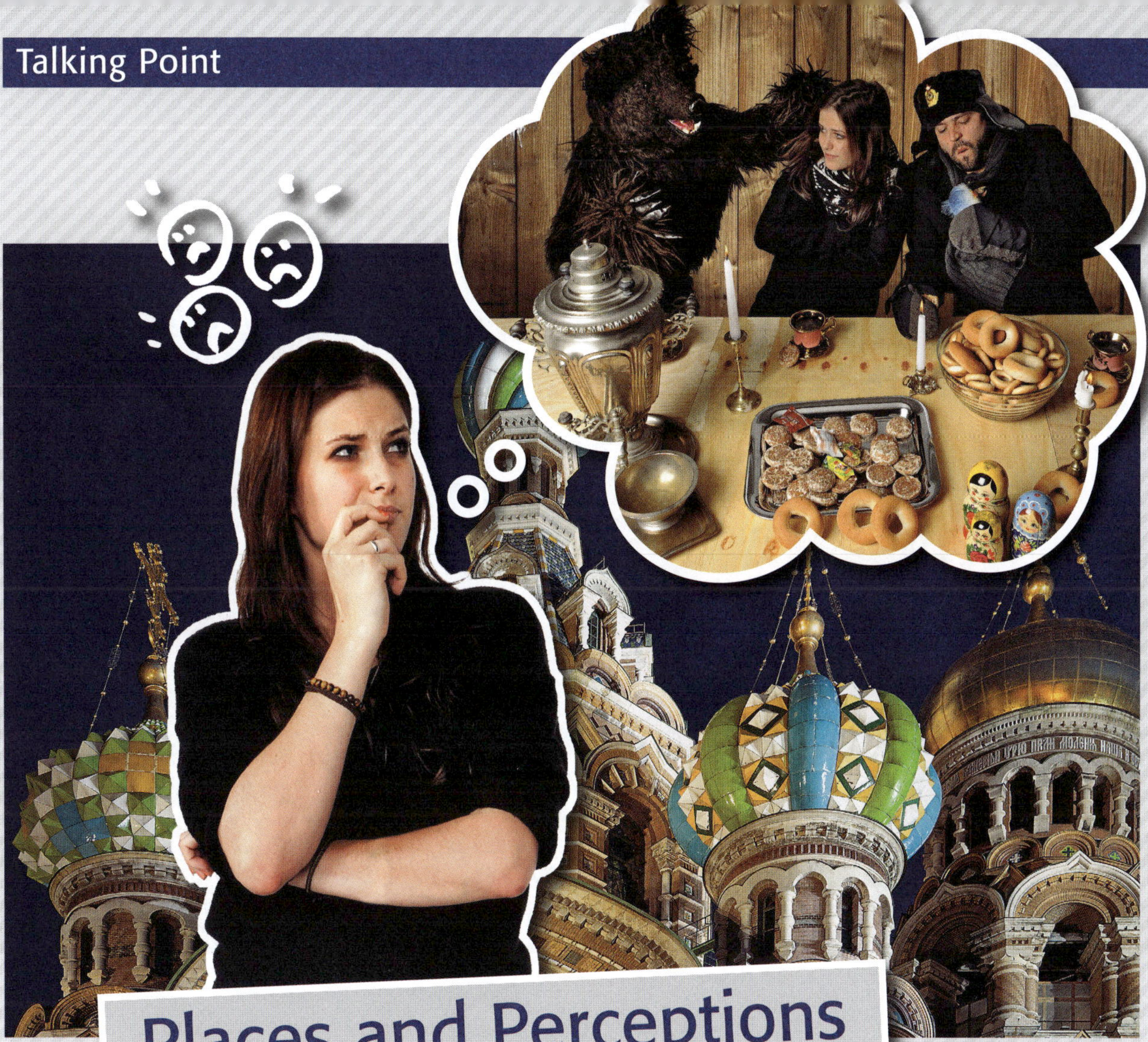

Talking Point

Places and Perceptions

1
We all have preconceived ideas about places we've never been to. The media and other people's anecdotes all help us to imagine countries, cities and regions we've never visited ourselves.

Our ideas about unfamiliar places are also shaped by stereotypes. Whether we like it or not, it's these old-fashioned, simplistic ideas – both positive and negative – that can have the strongest influence on how places are perceived by outsiders.

2
Talk about a place you went to that was different from your first ideas about it. Explain how it was different and say whether you were positively surprised or disappointed. You could also discuss where your ideas came from before your visit. Did they come from stereotypes?

3
Talk about a country, city or region you know well that has a stereotypical reputation. Sum up its reputation, then discuss how true or untrue these ideas are.

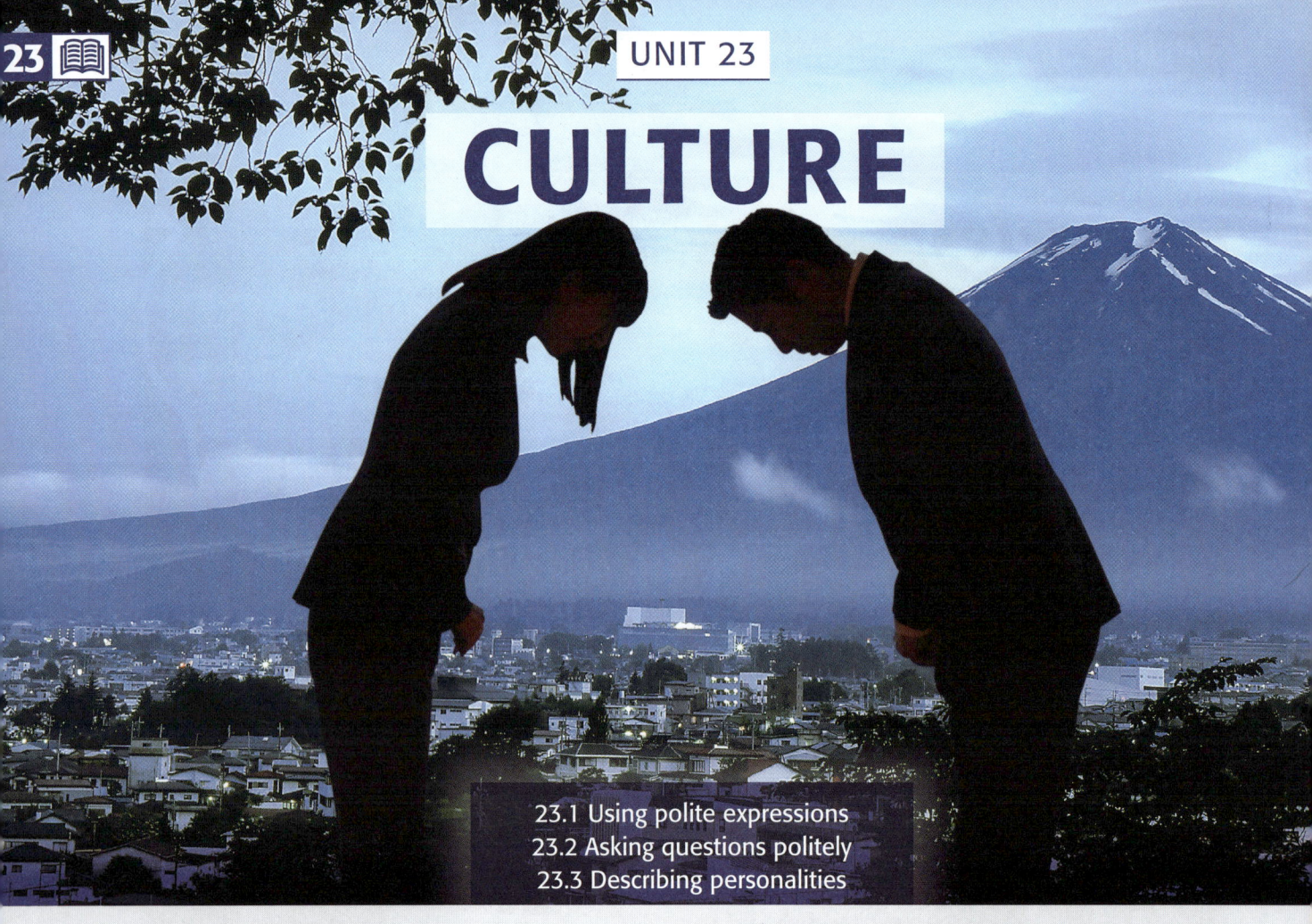

UNIT 23
CULTURE

23.1 Using polite expressions
23.2 Asking questions politely
23.3 Describing personalities

23.1 Reading

Polite expressions	When to use them
Excuse me.	Say this to get someone's attention – e.g. to stop someone in the street.
Sorry. Sorry about (that). Sorry I'm late.	Use these expressions to apologize – e.g. if you fail to arrive on time for an appointment, or if you accidentally bump into someone.
Excuse me? Sorry? Pardon me?	Use these phrases – with rising intonation (like in a question) – if you didn't hear what someone said.
Good morning. Good afternoon. Good evening.	These greetings can be used instead of "Hello" and "Hi" at specific times of day.
Thanks. Thank you. Thanks a lot. Thanks very much. Thank you very much.	These related expressions are used to say that you're grateful. As a simple rule, the longer the phrase, the more grateful you sound.
You're welcome.	You can use this reply after someone has thanked you.
No problem.	You can use this reply after someone has said sorry for something.
After you.	Say this if you open a door for someone, to invite them to go before you.
Bye. Goodbye. See you (later/soon).	Use these when parting.

23.2 Reading

From: Elliot Jennings
To: oliver.hewitt@allnetway.com
Subject: Culture
Attachment: –

Dear Oliver,

I hope you're well. I'm not sure if you remember me. We met when you came to our offices a few weeks ago. We had quite a long (and very interesting) chat about your experiences of working in Japan. It's on this subject that I'm writing to you. I wonder if you could give me a bit of advice? I'm going to Tokyo in a couple of weeks to see a client there. It'll be my first visit to Japan. So I wanted to ask you if you could give me a few tips.

My main worry is how to greet people. Can you tell me whether I should bow? I once read that there's a very specific way to do it and that you should bow in different ways depending on the person you're meeting. So I don't know if I should do it at all. I'm not sure whether it's better to just shake hands and avoid the problem. Do you know if that's acceptable for Westerners?

Many thanks in advance for any advice you can give me.

Elliot Jennings

23.3 Reading

CHARACTERISTICS AND CULTURE: A QUESTION OF JUDGMENT

We all know that behavior depends on culture. The cultures of countries, regions, families, companies and groups of friends all affect the way people behave. So it's easy to think that people from particular cultures have particular characteristics.

In fact, it's more correct to say that, in different cultures, people's characteristics are judged differently. An example: Imagine, in Country A, an employee takes 30 minutes for lunch each day, has no other breaks and spends only a little time chatting to colleagues, cracking jokes. In Country A, he's described as hardworking, reliable and funny. However, when this person moves abroad to work in Country B, which has different cultural values, his character is described very differently. A local colleague says he's fairly quiet – not exactly shy, but not very friendly. Then during the brief moments when he's not working, his behavior is rather strange – to the local colleague, he suddenly seems too relaxed and rather silly.

The local colleague is hardworking and reliable, too – at least, in the perception of Country B. There, you can take a two-hour lunch break, and still be seen as hardworking. However, if this colleague moved to Country A, she might be described as lazy. And her more serious manner in conversation might make her seem a bit boring.

23

23.1 Listening (Track 26)

You're going to hear six people making comments in different situations. Listen and think of suitable replies using polite expressions. Write down the expressions you choose below.

1.
2.
3.
4.
5.
6.

23.2 Listening (Track 27)

Part A The questions in A (1–4 below) are direct. Rephrase them in B to make them less direct and more polite.

1. A: Is there a subway station near here?
   B: Excuse me. Do you know if _____?

2. A: When's the next bus?
   B: Excuse me. Can you tell me _____?

3. A: What time is it?
   B: Excuse me. Do you know _____?

4. A: Is this ticket still valid?
   B: Excuse me. Can you tell me whether _____?

Part B Now listen and check your answers.

23.3 Listening (Track 28)

Part A You're going to hear an interview with Jo Merino, an expert in intercultural relations. She's going to discuss how people from two different cultures show that they're friendly. Listen, then sum up what she says. Use the key words from the interview below to help you.

Culture 1: open share friend
Culture 2: respect uncomfortable invasive

Part B Compare the examples discussed by Jo Merino with the way people behave in your culture and in other cultures you know about.

49

23.1 Follow-up

Write polite expressions that are suitable for each situation below. Then look at the table in Reading 23.1 and check your answers.

1. You didn't hear what somebody said.
2. Somebody thanks you, and you reply.
3. You want to stop somebody in the street.
4. Somebody bumps into you and apologizes, and you reply.
5. You don't arrive on time for an appointment, and apologize.
6. You leave somebody, but will see the person again in the evening.
7. Somebody gives you a gift. You want to show that you're extremely grateful.
8. You open a door for somebody and invite the person to go through before you.

23.2 Follow-up

Rephrase the questions below. Then compare them with the questions in the email in Reading 23.2.

1. Could you give me a bit of advice? – I wonder _____?
2. Could you give me a few tips? – I wanted to ask you _____.
3. Should I bow? – Can you tell me _____?
4. Is it better to just shake hands and avoid the problem? – I'm not sure _____.
5. Is that acceptable for Westerners? – Do you know _____?

23.3 Follow-up

Answer these questions about the article in Reading 23.3.

1. The text mentions countries, regions, families, companies and friends. How are these examples linked to the topic of the article?
2. What point does the article make about judgment?
3. In Country A, people think the employee is hard-working. How might this characteristic be judged in Country B?
4. People think the employee is funny in Country A. How do judgments about this change in Country B?
5. In a culture where humor is important (like Country A in the article), how might people describe somebody who's serious?

23.1 Language Summary — Using polite expressions

Excuse me. I'm looking for the nearest subway station.
Excuse me? / Sorry? / Pardon me? I didn't hear what you said.
Did I stand on your foot? Sorry. / Sorry about that.
Sorry I'm late. I got stuck in traffic. – No problem.

Thanks.
Thank you.
Thanks a lot.
Thanks very much.
Thank you very much.

Thank you. – You're welcome.

→ LANGUAGE PRACTICE 23.1 > PAGE 108

23.2 Language Summary — Asking questions politely

Do you know where the station is?
Can you tell me if there's a train to the airport?

- I wonder
- I don't know   if that would be OK.
- I'm not sure   whether that's possible.
- I wanted to ask

→ LANGUAGE PRACTICE 23.2 → PAGE 108

23.3 Language Summary — Describing personalities

She's not much fun to be with.
She doesn't talk much.
She doesn't enjoy meeting new people.
She's easy to get to know and get along with.
She always does what she promises to do.
She makes us laugh.
She doesn't get stressed.
She doesn't have much of a sense of humor.
She doesn't like working.
She works hard.

She's
- boring.
- quiet.
- shy.
- friendly.
- reliable.
- funny.
- relaxed.
- serious.
- lazy.
- hard-working.

→ LANGUAGE PRACTICE 23.3 → PAGE 109

Talking Point

Culture Shock

1
According to the dictionary, culture shock is "the feeling of disorientation experienced by a person suddenly subjected to an unfamiliar culture or way of life".

Culture shock can hit tourists on vacation, employees whose firms merge with foreign companies, and even diners in foreign restaurants in their home town. They say travel broadens the mind. Culture shock blows your mind.

2
Using your experience and your imagination, come up with a list of examples of types of culture shock that can occur with international travel and/or international business. For example: food and drink, or the way people greet one another. Then compare your list with the one on the *Resource Sheet*.

3
Using your list and the one on the *Resource Sheet* for ideas, talk about any kind of culture shock you've experienced – or any interesting differences you've noticed between your culture and foreign cultures.

UNIT 24
EATING OUT

24.1 Talking about places to eat
24.2 Talking about menus
24.3 Using polite language at the table

24.1 Reading

EATING OUT
NEAR THE HOTEL

Whether you're looking for a quick bite from a snack bar or planning a three-course dinner at an exclusive restaurant, you'll find a great choice of places to eat just a short walk from the hotel.

Check out our recommendations below. And don't hesitate to ask at the front desk for more details. Our staff will be happy to advise you and, if required, call a restaurant and reserve a table for you.

K3 Mall
The food court at the K3 shopping mall offers a wide range of fast-food outlets. *Lunch Line*, a self-service buffet on the first floor of the mall, provides a good choice of hot meals and salads.

Jaipur
Just across from the hotel, Jaipur serves a selection of Indian dishes. Takeouts can also be ordered.

24.2 Reading

~~Understanding English menus~~ Using English to understand menus

Often, it's impossible to translate the names of dishes on foreign menus into English. So learning how to understand "English menus" isn't always helpful if you're using English internationally. It's often more useful to know the English needed to *explain* dishes. That way, you can understand the explanations on the English version of a foreign menu (if available). Or you can ask the waiter, or the local friends or colleagues you're dining with, for explanations (if they speak English). If you're the host, you can explain the menu, in English, to your foreign friends or colleagues who don't speak the local language.

It also makes sense to accept that you'll never learn all the words needed to *describe* every type of food. Instead, there are some helpful words and phrases you can use to describe types of food, when you don't know the word in English. Some examples:

> *This is a seafood dish. I'm not sure how to say it in English. It's a type of shellfish…*

> *This is a vegetarian dish. In it, there are … how do you say it in English? It's a kind of vegetable. It's about this big. It can be red or green or yellow.*

> *This is a sort of curry. It's not too spicy.*

24.3 Reading

Surviving at the dinner table in English

Normally, there's nothing more enjoyable than having a relaxing dinner, either in a restaurant with friends or colleagues, or as a guest at someone's home. However, when you're in a foreign country, the experience can be stressful. And not just because of the culture shock. If you're speaking English as a second language, talking at the dinner table can be challenging. One reason for this problem is that meals take time.

A conversation over dinner might last an hour or more. During this time, the discussion will be very unpredictable. This will test your vocabulary, as the conversation continually jumps from one subject to another. It will also test your comprehension skills as you try to keep up with the discussion.

Of course, there's no quick way to improve your comprehension skills and vocabulary knowledge. Although it is possible to quickly learn some useful phrases to help you "survive" at the dinner table. These will allow you to do the following:

– Use suitable expressions when you're passing and serving food and drinks.
– Make compliments about the food, in order to be polite to your host.
– Talk to the waiter in a foreign restaurant (if he or she speaks English).

24.1 Listening (Track 29)

Part A You're going to hear a discussion at a hotel front desk. A guest is asking for some information about places to eat. Listen, then answer the questions below.

1. What meal does the guest want to have? QUICK lunch
2. Does the guest want to have a takeout? SIT DOWN
3. What place does the receptionist suggest? IT'S A SELF SERVICE BUFFET
4. What point does the receptionist make about the time of day? IT'S BUSY

Part B Use the words below to complete the sentences from the discussion.

~~busy~~   ~~quiet~~   ~~service~~   ~~take out~~   ~~tray~~   ~~waiters~~

1. Do you want to sit down to eat or get a snack to **TAKE OUT**?
2. Is there anywhere where the **SERVICE** is fairly fast?
3. They have a self-service buffet – there are no **WAITERS**.
4. You just take a **TRAY**, get what you want, then go and pay.
5. It gets **BUSY** there at lunchtime – it's very popular.
6. But it should be fairly **QUIET** now – it's quite early.

24.2 Listening (Track 30)

Underline the syllable that's stressed. Then listen and check.

1. seafood
2. poultry
3. vegetarian
4. spicy
5. alcohol
6. appetizer
7. dessert
8. portion
9. menu

24.3 Listening (Track 31)

Part A You're going to hear five short dialogues during meals. Listen and match each dialogue to one of the descriptions in A–C.

1. ___
2. ___
3. ___
4. ___
5. ___

A Passing and serving food and drinks
B Making compliments about the food
C Dealing with the waiter

Part B Underline the correct highlighted words to complete these sentences from the dialogues. Then choose the correct replies from A–C below

1. Would you like / mind / able to passing me the salt, please?
2. Would it be able / possible / mind to have a knife and fork?
3. Would anybody like / mind / want some more?

A Yes, please.   B Here you are.   C No problem.

Part C Look at the transcript on page 136. Can you find seven words for things that are often found on tables at mealtimes?

_____

24.1 Follow-up

Look at the extract from a hotel brochure in Reading 24.1. Find the names of places in the brochure that match the descriptions below.

1 a classy, expensive place to eat
2 an indoor place where you can sit down to eat, which has several different food outlets around it
3 you help yourself to food (there are no waiters), then take it to your table to eat it
4 a place where you buy food to take home
5 a place where you can go for a quick meal

24.2 Follow-up

Complete the sentences below. You could look at the article in Reading 24.2 to help you.

1 Sometimes, you can't translate foreign dishes into English. You have to
2 A shellfish is a type of
3 A dish that doesn't have meat in it is called a
4 A well-known characteristic of curry is that it tastes
5 A pepper is a vegetable that can have three different colors:

24.3 Follow-up

Look at the descriptions in 1–3. Below each one, write two or three sentences as examples of what people might say at the table.

1 Expressions for passing and serving food and drink

2 Making compliments about the food

3 Talking to the waiter

24.1 Language Summary — Talking about places to eat

It's a busy restaurant. It's a good idea to `reserve a table`.
It's a three-`course` meal, with a `starter` / an `appetizer`, a `main course` and a `dessert`.
Have you had time to look at the `menu`? Are you ready to `order`?
I was surprised when I got the `bill/check`. The meal was really expensive.
It says $65. Is `service included`? Or do we need to `leave a tip` for the waiter?
It's an `exclusive restaurant` – very classy, but very expensive.
It's not really a restaurant. It's just a `snack bar`. They just sell snacks.
They sell burgers and fried chicken and things like that. It's a `fast-food` place.
There are no waiters. You get your own food from the `buffet`. It's `self-service`.
Are you OK carrying those plates? Would you like a `tray` to put them on?
The waiters are so good in that restaurant. `The service` is excellent.

→ LANGUAGE PRACTICE 24.1 → PAGE 109

24.2 Language Summary — Talking about menus

I'm not sure how to say this in English. / How do you say it in English?
It's a type/kind/sort of
- `vegetable`.
- `fruit`.
- `meat`.
- `fish`.
- `seafood`.
- `shellfish`.

I don't eat meat. I'm a `vegetarian`.
It's a `soft drink`. It's not an `alcoholic drink`.

→ LANGUAGE PRACTICE 24.2 → PAGE 109

24.3 Language Summary — Using polite language at the table

`Would you mind passing me` the sauce? – Here you are.
`Would it be possible to have` some more bread?
`Would anybody like` more water?

Things on the table

`knife (knives)`, `fork`, `spoon`, `chopsticks`
`plate`, `dish`, `glass`, `cup`
`salt` `and` `pepper`

→ LANGUAGE PRACTICE 24.3 → PAGE 109

Talking Point
(Track 32)

Restaurants: Recipes for Success

1

What makes a restaurant successful? It goes without saying that the food must be good. Though, clearly, there are lots of other important "ingredients".

Think about your experiences – both good and bad – of eating out. Discuss some of the things that made you like or dislike different restaurant meals you've had.

2

Come up with a list of points that, in your opinion, make the difference between a good restaurant and one that's not so good. Then, compare your list with the one on the *Resource Sheet*.

3

In a moment, you're going to hear an interview with Harry Ingham, a chef who owns two popular restaurants. He's going to say which one of the points on the *Resource Sheet* he thinks is the most important "ingredient" for a successful restaurant. Before listening, discuss what you think he might say.

Listen to the interview, then sum up what Harry Ingham says. Compare his opinions with the points you discussed before.

4

Talk about some well-known restaurant chains that are popular internationally and/or in your country. Why do you think they've been successful?

UNIT 25
CONSUMER SOCIETY

25.1 Understanding advertisements
25.2 Discussing precautions
25.3 Describing trends

17 Sep. 2019

25.1 Reading

SALE Ends **January 28**

SPECIAL OFFER 25% OFF

HALF-PRICE FARES*
LIMITED SEATS AVAILABLE
BOOK NOW
*See conditions below

WIN A CARIBBEAN CRUISE

SUBSCRIBE **NOW** AND CLAIM YOUR **FREE GIFT.**

ONE FREE
BUY ONE GET ONE **FREE**

25.2 Reading

FROM SALESPERSON TO SALES ADVISOR
BUT HOW GOOD IS SALES ADVICE?

"Salesperson" is an unloved job title. It has a pushy image. This stereotype may be unfair, but it explains why the title is going out of fashion. Today, increasingly, companies employ, not salespeople, but friendlier-sounding "sales advisors" or "sales consultants". Sometimes, the word "sales" is removed altogether to give titles such as "customer advisor".

However, customers should be careful. It's important not to confuse advising and selling. Yes, "customer advisors" can offer valuable help with some things – for example, explaining technical information about products. But it's important to remember that they might not give the best buying advice. One reason is that sales staff sometimes earn higher commissions for selling some products and lower commissions for others (depending on how much profit the company makes on different items). So they might just try to sell the product that will pay the highest commission, rather than the one that's best suited to the customer's needs. Therefore, take care. Think twice before accepting "customer advice". It's dangerous to see a commercial salesperson as an independent advisor. Make sure you remember who you're dealing with.

25.3 Reading

Could the rise in food prices improve our eating habits?

News
HAS THE GROWTH OF UNLIMITED CALLS REDUCED THE AVERAGE PHONE BILL?

Is the recent drop in burglaries due to a fall in the price of electrical goods?

Today
AS THE PRICE OF OIL INCREASES, SHOULD FUEL TAXES DECREASE?

25

25.1 Listening (Track 33)

Part A You're going to hear Hanna Trent, an advertising executive, discussing the questions below. Before listening, try to answer them yourself. You'll need to look at the six advertisements in Reading 25.1.

- What message is given by all six ads? — 25% off
- What other message is in three of the ads?

— DON'T DELAY
BUY QUICKLY
— HURRY!

Part B Now listen to Hanna Trent. What does she say about the questions above? Compare her explanations with the points you discussed in Part A.

25.2 Listening (Track 34)

Part A You're going to hear two people giving advice on how to make the best choice when buying expensive things (e.g. TV sets, washing machines, large pieces of furniture) from stores. Before listening, discuss your views on this question. What advice would you give?

Part B Now listen. What advice does each person give? Make notes and compare it with your advice from Part A.

Advice from Person 1

Advice from Person 2

25.3 Listening (Track 35)

Reword the sentences about trends, below, using get. Then listen and check your answers.

1. When new TVs come out, the price of older models falls.
   When new TVs come out, older models _____ (get).
2. Most experts predict that in the long-term, the price of oil will rise.
   Most experts predict that in the long-term, oil will _____ (get).
3. Over the years, the technology used in cars has improved.
   Over the years, the technology used in cars has _____ (gotten).
4. As furniture has become cheaper, its quality has decreased.
   As furniture has become cheaper, its quality has _____ (gotten).
5. The global market for cell phones is growing.
   The global market for cell phones is _____ (getting).

25.1 Follow-up

Find suitable advertising words and expressions to match 1–3. Then look at the ads in Reading 25.1 and check your answers.

1 50% reduction

50% _____

_____ - _____

Buy one get one _____

2 temporarily low prices

_____ _____

3 a present you don't have to pay for

_____ _____

25.2 Follow-up

Answer these questions about the article in Reading 25.2.

1 Why do some companies call their sales staff "sales advisors", "sales consultants" or "customer advisors"?

2 What example is given in the article of some useful advice that salespeople can offer customers?

3 According to the article, why don't salespeople always give customers the best buying advice?

4 What's the main piece of advice given by the article?

25.3 Follow-up

Write a paragraph in reply to one of the questions in the newspaper clippings in Reading 25.3. It should explain your opinion and the reasons for your point of view. You could use the phrases below to help you.

- I (don't) think it's true that … .
- In my opinion, … .
- The reason for my opinion is that … .

25.1 Language Summary — Understanding advertisements

Advertisements are sometimes called ads for short.
The purpose of ads is to advertise products. They're for advertising.
Ads on the TV and on the radio are often called commercials.
Sometimes, stores have sales, when they sell things at lower prices for a short time.
When a product is on sale for a lower price for a short time, it's called a special offer.
If a price is reduced by 25%, the packaging will say 25% off.
If a price is reduced by 50%, the packaging will often say half-price.
Most special offers only last for a short time. They're for a limited period.
Special offers often propose an extra quantity of a product for free or offer a free gift.

→ LANGUAGE PRACTICE 25.1 → PAGE 110

25.2 Language Summary — Discussing precautions

Be careful.
Take care.

Make sure you
Make sure you don't

It's important to ▶ do that.
It's important not to

It's dangerous to

→ LANGUAGE PRACTICE 25.2 → PAGE 110

25.3 Language Summary — Describing trends

| to increase | to rise | to grow | |
| an increase | a rise | growth | |

| to decrease | to fall | to drop | to reduce |
| a decrease | a fall | a drop | a reduction |

to get better — to improve / an improvement

to get worse

→ LANGUAGE PRACTICE 25.3 → PAGE 110

Talking Point

Advertising Impact

1

In recent years, the world's companies have spent between $400 billion and $500 billion annually on advertising. For the global population of seven billion people, that's a rough average of $60 to $70 per person. In rich countries, the amount is far higher.

The conclusion is clear: We're bombarded by advertising. In fact, there's so much of it – on the street, on TV, on the web, in newspapers and magazines, on the radio – that we don't notice most of it. Think for a moment. As a rough guess, how many ads or commercials do you think you've been exposed to in the last seven days? How many of them got your attention?

2

Discuss these questions about advertising:
- Think of a recent ad or commercial that got your attention. Why did you notice it?
- Think of an ad you remember from years ago. What made it memorable?

Based on the points you just discussed, what do you think makes certain ads or commercials successful?

3

Different styles of advertising are used for different types of products and services. Describe the styles of ads and commercials for the products and services on the *Resource Sheet 25C*. Give specific examples of ads you can remember.

Grammar Summary 21–25

Compounds of *some*, *any*, *no* and *every*

We can use the following words with some, any, no and every:

body/one	to talk about people	▶ I know somebody/someone who's an actor.
thing	to talk about things	▶ I haven't had anything to eat this morning.
where	to talk about places	▶ I searched for my keys everywhere in the house.

We use any in questions, and with negative forms such as don't, isn't or haven't:

Question: Do you know anybody who speaks Russian?
Negative: I haven't had anything to drink.

We can also use any to mean "It doesn't matter who/which/where".

Where shall we go to eat? – I don't mind. We can go anywhere you like.
You can bring a guest of your choice. You can invite anybody you want to.

Indirect questions

Indirect questions start with an introduction (see below). Often, the introduction is used to make the question sound more polite. This is because, in some cultures, it is impolite to be too direct.

Introductions to indirect questions

▶ Could you tell me … ?
▶ Do you know … ?
▶ I wanted to ask … ?

With indirect questions, change the word order in the same way as with reported speech (see Grammar Summary 16–20).

Direct question	Indirect question
Where's the bus stop?	Could you tell me where the bus stop is?
Is there a bus stop near here?	Do you know if there's a bus stop near here?

be able to, *could* and *managed to*

We use will / won't be able to to mean can / can't in the future:

Present	Future
I can meet him now.	I'll be able to meet him next week.

We can use was(n't) / were(n't) able to to mean can / can't in the past.

Present	Past
I can meet him now.	I was able to meet him last week.

We can use could to say what was possible in the past. Normally, we only use could to talk about past situations that lasted a long time.

I used to live near my office, so I could walk to work every day.

We use managed to (not could) to say what was possible when we talk about past events.

I lost my keys, but after searching the house ▶ I managed to find them.
Not ▶ I could find them.

We use didn't manage to or couldn't to say what wasn't possible when we talk about past events.

    I lost my keys. I searched the house, but I didn't manage to find them.
or I lost my keys. I searched the house, but I couldn't find them.

Vocabulary Summary 21–25

Social issues

health	drugs	real estate	out of work
hospital	crime	to rent (a home)	the cost of living
doctor	to steal	homeless	the climate
nurse	violence	the economy	education
medical care	police officer	recession	pollution
patient	jail	unemployment	

City attractions

museum	cafe	theater	concert
art gallery	bar	opera	sports stadium
statue	takeout	ballet	

Polite language

Excuse me.	Pardon me?	Thank you.	No problem.
Sorry (about that).	Good morning.	Thanks a lot.	After you.
Sorry I'm late.	Good afternoon.	Thanks very much.	Bye.
Excuse me?	Good evening.	Thank you very much.	Goodbye.
Sorry?	Thanks.	You're welcome.	See you (later/soon).

Personal characteristics

hard-working	quiet	relaxed	serious
reliable	shy	silly	boring
funny	friendly	lazy	

Eating out

to reserve a table	main course	to leave a tip	self-service
waiter	to order	snack bar	buffet
menu	dessert	exclusive restaurant	takeout
course	check/bill	food court	
appetizer/starter	service is included	fast food	

Types of food and drink

seafood	spicy	fish	alcohol
shellfish	vegetarian	fruit	alcoholic drink
vegetable	meat	(fruit) juice	
curry	poultry	soft drink	

Advertising

advertisement	commercial	…% off	to subscribe
ad	sale	half-price	see conditions
to advertise	special offer	limited	the small print

Trends

to/an increase	to/a fall	an improvement	to grow
to/a decrease	to/a drop	to reduce	growth
to/a rise	to improve	a reduction	

Skills Summary 21–25

After Units 21 to 25, you can ...

Skill	Section
▶ refer to problems	21.1
▶ discuss possibilities	21.1
▶ make suggestions	21.2
▶ respond to suggestions	21.2
▶ discuss problems in the past	21.3
▶ discuss solutions in the past	21.3
▶ refer to commonly discussed social issues	22.1
▶ refer to unspecified people	22.2
▶ refer to unspecified places	22.2
▶ refer to unspecified things	22.2
▶ talk about city entertainment	22.3
▶ talk about city recreation	22.3
▶ use appropriate polite expressions	23.1
▶ phrase questions politely	23.2
▶ refer to personal characteristics	23.3
▶ talk about food outlets	24.1
▶ explain dishes	24.2
▶ refer to types of food	24.2
▶ make polite requests	24.3
▶ refer to objects on the dinner table	24.3
▶ understand offers in advertisements	25.1
▶ explain precautions	25.2
▶ emphasize importance	25.2
▶ describe positive changes	25.3
▶ describe negative changes	25.3

UNIT 26

MONEY

26.1 Discussing money matters
26.2 Discussing money matters in the past
26.3 Giving precise and approximate figures

26.1 Reading

CRYSTAL CLEAR

Every week, Crystal Clear explains a confusing financial topic in simple terms. This week: the subprime mortgage crisis.

Before 2008, the safest place to keep your money was in a bank account. Then the global banking crisis hit, causing a "run" on a bank. After rumors that the British bank Northern Rock could fail, panicking customers waited in line to withdraw their savings, in cash. Soon after, the American bank Lehman Brothers went bankrupt, and the global banking system began to collapse. Governments had to step in to save the day.

The cause of the crisis began in the booming American real-estate market. Banks were lending money to so-called "subprime" customers. This was the name for people with a low credit rating – that is, people who had a high risk of not repaying their loans. Generally, these mortgages had very low interest rates for the first year or two, so customers were able to keep up their monthly repayments. But then these rates increased, monthly payments went up and customers suddenly found that they weren't able to repay the money they'd borrowed.

As a result, many subprime customers lost their homes, as the banks seized and sold them to recover their money – a procedure called foreclosure. However, the trouble was, real-estate prices began to fall, so many homes were worth less than the money borrowed to buy them. As a result, the banks couldn't recover the money they'd lent. Then, as the number of foreclosures increased, more homes went on the market, prices fell more, and things went from bad to worse.

26.2 Reading

Real Estate Prices

Back in 2007, I sold my apartment for double the price I paid for it in 1998. When I bought the place, I thought it cost a fortune. But it was easy to get a mortgage at the time – the bank lent me the money without any problem. Then, just after that, real-estate prices shot up. I think they rose by a 100% in six or seven years. It was a crazy time – there was so much demand. I remember, I put my apartment on the market and within one week I got three offers for it.

So I made a lot of money on the sale – and at the same time, I withdrew my money from the market. Then I rented another apartment while I was looking for a new home, as it was difficult to find places – as I said, there was so much demand. And then, suddenly the real-estate bubble burst. That was it. Prices fell. So I just waited. I knew there was no point buying in a falling market. In the end, I waited three and a half years. Eventually, I found a house I really liked, so I took the opportunity and went for it. I spent about 30% less than it was worth in 2007. That was in 2010, so it was before prices hit rock bottom. I guess the house lost some value just after that – but not too much.

So here's some advice from someone who won in the real-estate lottery: buy at the bottom of the market, sell at the top, wait for prices to fall, then buy again. And the key to perfect timing? Luck!

26.3 Reading

THE COLOR OF MONEY IS YELLOW

The first decade of the 21st century left investors feeling off color, after global markets gave them the wildest rollercoaster ride in financial history. Over that period, the total value of the world's most famous stock market index, the Dow Jones Industrial Average, went from 11,497 at the end of 1999 – via a high of 14,164 in 2007 and a low of 6,547 in 2009 – to close the decade at 10,428. The end result was that, from the start of 2000 to the start of 2010, the Dow lost 9.3%.

Therefore, the value of "working money" – finance that was put to work in companies – actually fell across the decade. Paradoxically, over the same period the price of gold – "dead money" piled in bank vaults – rose by about 400%. Gold also did better than oil: the price of "black gold" increased by 300% in that decade. It beat wheat, too. The cereal grew in value by roughly 250%.

The rise in the price of "useless" gold is surprising when you compare it with useful commodities, such as wheat. Some more figures show just how extraordinary the value of the yellow metal is.

In 2010, the total weight of gold extracted from the earth in the whole of history was just over 150,000 tons – a quantity that would fit into less than four Olympic-sized swimming pools.

At the same time, that quantity of metal had a total value of more than $6,000,000,000,000. By contrast, global wheat production totals nearly 650,000,000 tons per year – which, at US prices, has a total value of almost $400,000,000,000. Therefore, all the world's gold is approximately 1,500% more valuable than the world's wheat – even though the total weight of gold is just 0.023% that of wheat.

26

26.1 Listening (Track 36)

Part A How serious would the consequences be for you if your bank failed and the government couldn't afford to save it? In a moment, you're going to hear a man's opinion on this question. But first give your own views.

Part B Now listen to the man. In the interview, he uses the verb "owe" three times. Use this word, and the words below, to sum up his opinion.

mortgage   savings   overall

26.2 Listening (Track 37)

Listen to the audio version of the blog about real-estate prices in Reading 26.2. In it, there are 23 irregular words for talking about the past (not including "was/were"). As you listen, write down as many of the words as you can.

26.3 Listening (Track 38–39)

Part A The numbers below are from the article in Reading 26.3. Write them in words. Then listen and check your answers.

1 the 21st century   century
2 (the year) 1999
3 14,164
4 (the year) 2007
5 9.3%   percent
6 150,000 tons   tons
7 $6,000,000,000,000   dollars
8 650,000,000 tons   tons
9 $400,000,000,000   dollars
10 0.023%   percent

Part B Now listen and complete these parts of the article, in figures. Then check your answers in Reading 26.3.

1 the Dow Jones Industrial Average went from _____ at the end of 1999
2 a low of _____ in 2009
3 to close the decade at _____
4 The cereal grew in value by roughly _____ %
5 gold is approximately _____ % more valuable than the world's wheat

26.1 Follow-up

Complete the explanations of the terms in 1–3. Use some or all of the words below. You could look at the article in Reading 26.1 to help you.

cash   loan   mortgage   repay   repayments   savings   withdraw

1 A run on a bank is when panicking customers
2 Subprime is a term used by banks to describe customers with a low credit rating – that is, people who have a high risk of
3 Foreclosure is when a bank seizes

26.2 Follow-up

Complete these extracts from the article in Reading 26.2. Use the correct past forms of the words.

1 I _____ (sell) my apartment for double the price I _____ (pay) for it in 1998.
2 When I _____ (buy) the place, I thought it _____ (cost) a fortune.
3 … the bank _____ (lend) me the money without any problem.
4 … real-estate prices _____ (shoot) up. I think they _____ (rise) by a 100%.
5 … I _____ (withdraw) my money from the market.
6 And then, suddenly, the real-estate bubble _____ (burst).
7 That was it. Prices _____ (fall).
8 I _____ (spend) about 30% less than it was worth in 2007.
9 I guess the house _____ (lose) some value just after that – but not too much.
10 So, here's some advice from someone who _____ (win) in the real-estate lottery.

26.3 Follow-up

Look at Reading 26.3. Are the sentences below true or false?

1 Between the ends of 1999 and 2009, oil did better than stocks.   T F
2 Stock prices never rose between 1999 and 2009.   T F
3 In one two-year period, the Dow Jones lost over half its value.   T F
4 Between 1999 and 2009, the price of gold rose more than oil.   T F
5 In 2010, the total value of the world's gold was about $6 billion.   T F
6 All the world's wheat is worth more than all the world's gold.   T F

26.1 Language Summary — Discussing money matters

People's monthly salaries are often paid directly into their bank account.
The money that people have kept is called savings. It's money they've saved.
When you take some of your money out of a bank, we say you withdraw money.
To buy a house or apartment, most people need to borrow money from a bank.
Money borrowed from a bank is called a loan.
Specifically, a loan used to buy a house or apartment is called a mortgage.
If the bank gives you a loan, we say the bank lends you money.
With a loan, you have to repay the money you've borrowed.
When you repay a loan, you also have to pay a percentage of interest.
If you have to repay money – for example, to a bank – we say you owe the bank money.
If people owe money, we say they have debts.

→ LANGUAGE PRACTICE 26.1 → PAGE 110

26.2 Language Summary — Discussing money matters in the past

Present	Past
sell	sold
pay	paid
buy	bought
cost	cost
spend	spent
lend	lent
win	won
lose	lost
withdraw	withdrew

→ LANGUAGE PRACTICE 26.2 → PAGE 111

26.3 Language Summary — Giving precise and approximate figures

I can't remember the exact price. It was ▶ about $500.
▶ roughly
▶ approximately

The price was $985. So it was ▶ nearly $1,000.
▶ almost

The price was $1,015. So it was ▶ just over $1,000.

Large numbers:
1,000,000 = one million
1,000,000,000 = one billion (= one thousand million)
1,000,000,000,000 = one trillion (= one thousand billion)

Decimals: 1.3056 = one point three zero five six

→ LANGUAGE PRACTICE 26.3 → PAGE 111

Talking Point

Million-Dollar Questions

1

How impressive is the title "millionaire"? It depends which country you live in. First, there's the question of currency. It's much easier to be a millionaire in Japanese yen than it is in US dollars or euros. Culture is an issue, too. In some countries, people admire wealth. In other places, they resent it. There are also different types of millionaire: those who are self-made, those who inherited their wealth, and a lucky few who won the lottery. This question of whether someone's millions were earned, given or won also influences how millionaires are viewed in different countries.

How are millionaires viewed in your country and in other countries you know about?

2

Discuss the questions below about self-made millionaires:
1. What drives certain people to make huge amounts of money?
2. What personal characteristics do you need to make a million?
3. What sacrifices do people often make on the road to riches?
4. How important is luck in making millions?

3

Does being rich make you happy? Discuss this question with regard to:
1. self-made millionaires
2. millionaires who inherited their wealth
3. people who won a fortune in the lottery

4

Imagine you won a fortune in a lottery. What would you do? "I wouldn't change as a person" is a common answer. But is that realistic?

UNIT 27
EMOTIONS

27.1 Describing positive feelings
27.2 Describing negative feelings
27.3 Linking and contrasting

27.1 Reading

THE CHEMISTRY OF SATISFACTION: TERRIFYING REACTIONS

We normally think of fear as a negative emotion. One of the most common expressions about fear is "scared to death". However, doing scary things – such as riding on rollercoasters – is one of the best ways to feel alive, thanks to two chemicals inside our bodies.

One of the substances is adrenaline, which is produced when we're frightened. And it's awesome stuff. Its main effect on the body is to increase our strength. This allows us to react more physically and extremely than we would normally be able to. It explains the expression "white-knuckle ride" – the adrenaline-powered grip during a rollercoaster ride which is so strong that blood is squeezed from your fingers as you hang on for dear life.

Adrenaline experiences are not always fun at the time. However, the real feeling of satisfaction comes afterwards, thanks to other chemicals called endorphins. These are produced after physical activity and generate a feeling of happiness. And if we overcame fear to do what we did, we also feel proud of ourselves – another positive feeling.

27.2 Reading

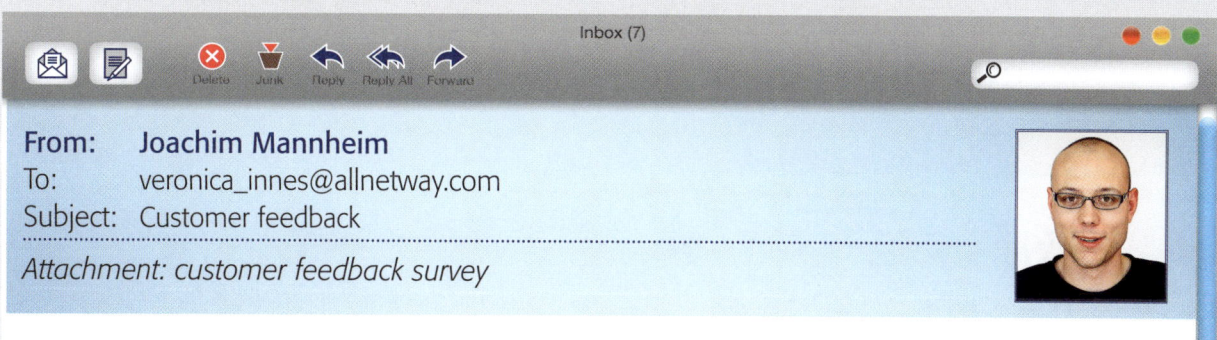

Dear Veronica,

Please find attached the customer feedback survey, as promised. It contains 138 feedback forms, which were completed during interviews with visitors in the first month after the amusement park opened.

The average customer rating is 5 out of 10. So the results are a bit disappointing. The low score might have something to do with the terrible weather we had last month. When the weather's awful, it's obvious that people feel more miserable. Also, at an amusement park, it's only natural that customers feel disappointed when it rains on their day out. However, we clearly can't blame everything on the rain.

As the next step, we need to find specific things that people criticized – especially things that several people complained about. One example is the problem of parking spaces. Quite a few customers were angry that they had to park on the grass, which quickly turned to mud in the heavy rain. I can certainly understand why people were annoyed about that. I went to the parking lot on the first day we opened, and was watching and feeling very embarrassed, as people had to walk through the mud to get to their cars.

27.3 Reading

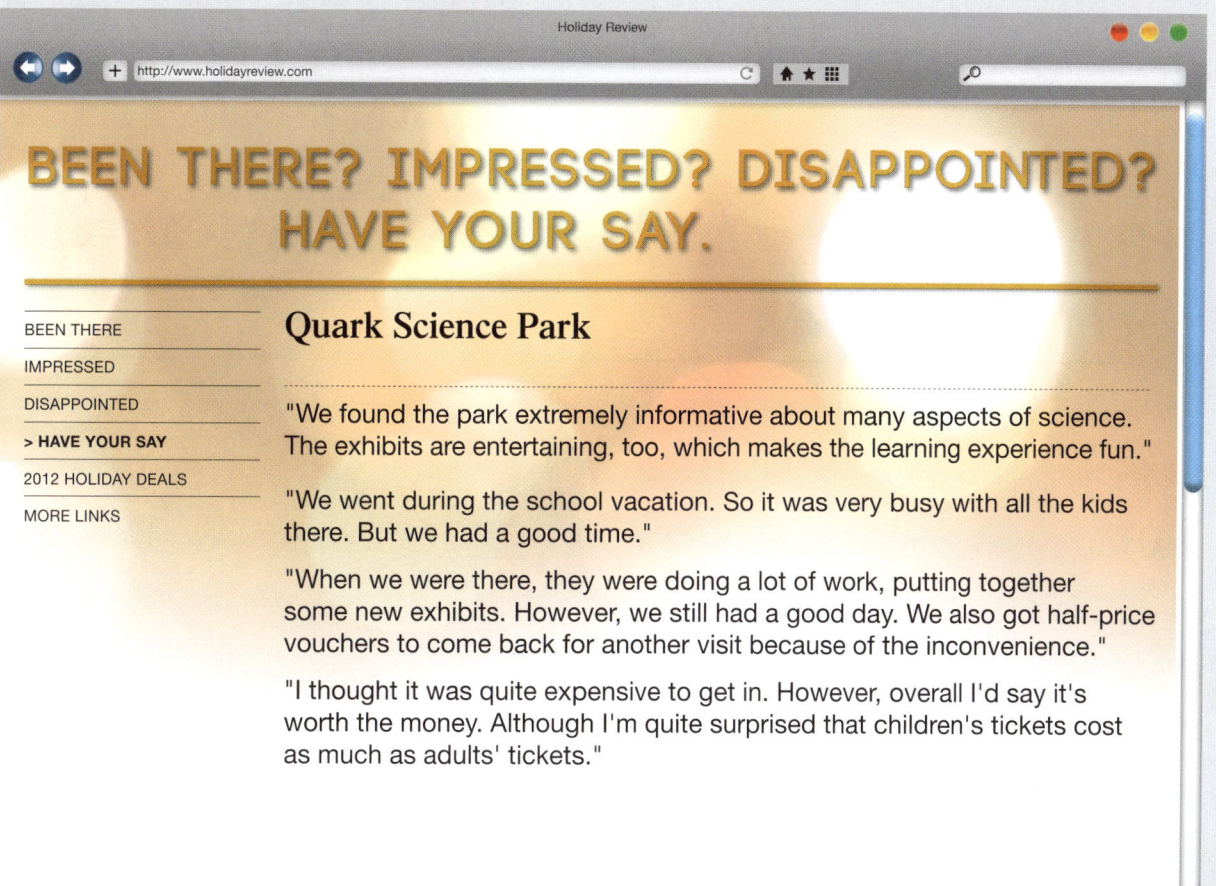

27.1 Listening (Track 40)

Part A You're going to hear four people describing their feelings just after riding on a rollercoaster. Listen for eight words that describe positive feelings. Write them below.

Part B When describing feelings about experiences, which words are used with "I'm …" and which are used with "(It) was …" ? Use the words above to complete the table below. Then listen again and check your answers.

It was _____.	It was _____.
It was _____.	I'm _____.
It was _____.	I'm _____.
It was _____.	I'm _____.

27.2 Listening (Track 41)

Part A You're going to hear a researcher asking a customer for her opinions about an amusement park. Listen, then sum up what the customer says.

Part B Choose three words in A–J that describe the customer's feelings.

A amused ☐
B annoyed ☐
C depressed ☐
D disappointed ☐
E embarrassed ☐
F frightened ☐
G nervous ☐
H proud ☐
I satisfied ☐
J surprised ☐

27.3 Listening (Track 42)

Look at 1–3. In the highlighted sentences on the right, how should the intonation in A and B be different? Practice saying the sentences. Then listen and compare your intonation with that in the recording.

1 A: I had a good day. The weather was good, too.
   B: I had a good day. But the weather wasn't very good.

2 A: The hotel was great. It was cheap, as well.
   B: The hotel was great. Although it was expensive.

3 A: There are tickets available. We also have some reduced fares.
   B: There are tickets available. However, we only have full-price fares.

27.1 Follow-up

Answer these questions about the article in Reading 27.1.

1. What expression is used to describe extreme fear?
2. When is adrenaline produced?
3. What does adrenaline do to people?
4. When are endorphins produced?
5. What feeling do endorphins give people?
6. How do people feel after they've overcome fear?

27.2 Follow-up

Look at the sentences about the situation discussed in the email in Reading 27.2. Choose the best word to complete each sentence.

annoyed   annoying   disappointed   disappointing   embarrassed   embarrassing

1. The survey results weren't as good as Joachim hoped. They're _____.
2. Visitors were angry that they had to walk through mud. They found it _____.
3. When the weather's bad, it's inevitable that visitors will be a bit _____.
4. Joachim watched visitors walking through the mud and felt _____.
5. When customers feel they haven't had value for money, they get _____.
6. When Joachim tells his boss about the poor results, it will be _____.

27.3 Follow-up

Use the words below to complete the extracts from Reading 27.3. You will need to use some words more than once. Sometimes, two different words are possible.

also   but   however   so   too

"We found the park extremely informative about many aspects of science. The exhibits are entertaining, 1 _____, which makes the learning experience fun."
"We went during the school vacation. 2 _____ it was very busy with all the kids there. 3 _____ we had a good time."
"When we were there, they were doing a lot of work, putting together some new exhibits. 4 _____, we still had a good day. We 5 _____ got half-price vouchers to come back for another visit because of the inconvenience."

27

27.1 Language Summary — Describing positive feelings

It was a great experience. It was
- brilliant !
- fantastic !
- awesome !

I'm happy that I did it. I'm
- glad .
- pleased .
- satisfied .

fun versus funny   We say something was fun when we enjoyed it.
We say something was funny when it made us laugh.

→ LANGUAGE PRACTICE 27.1 → PAGE 111

27.2 Language Summary — Describing negative feelings

It wasn't as good as I hoped.	= I was disappointed . It was disappointing .
I was angry.	= I was annoyed . It was annoying .
I was miserable.	= I was depressed . It was depressing .
I was ashamed.	= I was embarrassed . It was embarrassing .
It was really bad.	= It was terrible . It was awful .

→ LANGUAGE PRACTICE 27.2 → PAGE 111

27.3 Language Summary — Linking and contrasting

The food was good.   It was cheap,
- too .
- as well .

It was also cheap.

The food wasn't bad.   It wasn't expensive, either .

The food was good.
- But it was expensive.
- Although
- However ,

The trip was interesting and the weather was good. So we had a good time.

→ LANGUAGE PRACTICE 27.3 → PAGE 112

79

Talking Point

Stress: Psychology and Engineering

1

What, exactly, is stress? In engineering, it's defined as the amount of pressure that's pushing or pulling on an object. If there's too much stress compared with the strength of the material, the object will break.

What about stress with regard to emotions? How does the definition of stress in psychology compare with the definition in engineering?

2

In engineering, two ways to help cope with stress are:
- reduce the stress on materials (for example, by making the loads on them lighter)
- make materials stronger so they can cope with more stress without breaking

According to psychologists, the best techniques for coping with emotional stress are related to those used in engineering. Can you explain why this is true? Talk about different ways that people can:
- reduce the stress they're under.
- be emotionally stronger in order to cope better with stress.

After your discussion, compare your ideas with those on the *Resource Sheet*.

3

Now talk about the tips on the *Resource Sheet*. Which do you think are the best?

UNIT 28
ENTERTAINMENT

28.1 Talking about TV programs
28.2 Talking about music
28.3 Talking about stories

28.1 Reading

MORE AND MORE TV SHOWS ARE EXPORTED GLOBALLY
BUT HOW WELL DO THEY TRANSLATE?

In the age of digital communication, news travels around the planet in an instant. Thanks to satellite and cable television, it seems that every living room on earth has the same "TV window" on the world.

The phenomenon of globalized television goes beyond the news. Many of the famous faces on TV – Hollywood movie stars, pop stars and sports stars – are, of course, global celebrities. Even when stars are from the local country, frequently, the programs they appear in are imported concepts that are broadcast in dozens of countries around the world.

How well do TV programs really travel across borders? Movies, game shows, documentaries, comedies, reality TV shows – which types of show are the most suitable for making adaptations that can be exported? And which types often get lost in translation?

28.2 Reading

WHEN IT COMES TO GLOBALIZATION, NOTHING BEATS POP MUSIC

// MUSIC IS THE ULTIMATE EXPRESSION OF CULTURAL DIVERSITY. LOCAL STYLES OF MUSIC ARE CHARACTERIZED BY PARTICULAR INSTRUMENTS. AND LYRICS, AS POEMS IN THE LOCAL LANGUAGE, TELL STORIES THAT BELONG TO A NATIVE PEOPLE AND THEIR CULTURE. //

The above words, written more than 100 years ago, raise an interesting question. You'd think that tastes in music would be very different in different countries. In fact, pop music is the ultimate global product. It's not especially diverse; electric guitars and drums are by far the most common pop instruments. What's more, the lyrics are almost irrelevant; a high percentage of the global audience doesn't understand the language (primarily English) in which global pop songs are sung. //

The globalization of pop music also has nothing to do with the global media revolution. One of the best-selling global hits ever – with estimated sales of 25 million – is *Rock Around the Clock*, which the band Bill Haley and His Comets first recorded back in 1954. The huge international success of groups such as The Beatles in the 1960s also shows that music globalization is nothing new. So why has pop music been such a global success for so long? And has the success of international singers come at the expense of local talent in some countries?

28.3 Reading

THE BUILDING BLOCKS OF BLOCKBUSTER MOVIES

STORY
CHARACTERS
SCRIPT
ACTORS
SPECIAL EFFECTS

What makes a great movie?

Clearly, there are several important building blocks. The main one is obvious: The film must tell a good story. Then come the characters. The way the story develops depends on their personalities, on the relationships between them, and on how the main character changes as a result of the relationships and experiences he or she has in the story.

For many movies, the story and characters come from a novel, as many films are based on books.

The next step is for a screenwriter to turn the book into a script – a difficult task, as the full story told in a novel will almost always be too long for a movie. Having a great script is important for the next stage of development. If the script is good, there's a better chance of attracting the best actors to play the key parts. This will not only help the director to make a good movie; it will also help with marketing, as faces of big stars on movie posters are the best way of pulling in a big audience.

28

28.1 Listening (Track 43)

Part A You're going to hear Sabrina Esteras, a media consultant, talking about adapting TV programs for other countries. Listen, then answer the questions below.

1 According to Sabrina, what type of TV program is one of the easiest to adapt? *DOCUMENTARY*
2 What solutions can be used to adapt this type of program to the local language? *A – TRANSLATE WHAT / – DUBBED*
3 Which type of program is the most difficult to adapt to other languages? *COMEDIES, SHOW.*

Part B Look at the key words from the interview, below. Write a definition to explain what each word means.

1 presenter
2 narrator — *ONLY THE VOICE*
3 translate
4 subtitles
5 interpreter — *YOU NEED TO KNOW MORE*
6 dubbed (over)

28.2 Listening (Track 44)

Say the names of the musical instruments below. <u>Underline</u> the syllable that's stressed. Then listen and check your answers.

1 gui-tar
2 pi-a-no
3 vi-o-lin
4 trum-pet
5 sax-o-phone
6 ban-jo
7 re-cord-er
8 trom-bone
9 bag-pipes
10 ac-cor-di-on

28.3 Listening (Track 45–46)

Part A In a moment, you're going to hear a man talking about movies based on novels. He says what he thinks about watching a movie after you've read the novel it's based on. Before listening, give your opinion about what it's like to watch a movie about a novel you've read.

Part B Now listen to the man's views. Sum up what he says and compare his opinions with those you gave in Part A.

Part C Listen to the man discussing his experience of watching a famous movie trilogy – which is based on a novel trilogy – after reading the books. Then answer the questions below.

1 What's the man's overall opinion of the movies?

2 What four reasons does he give for his opinion?

3 Can you guess which movie trilogy he's talking about?

28.1 Follow-up

Complete the sentences below using suitable words. You could look at Reading 28.1 to help you.

1. Two ways of transmitting TV are via s_____ and via c_____.
2. The verb "to b_____" means to transmit TV programs.
3. A TV program about what's happening in the world is called the n_____.
4. Films are often called m_____.
5. The public can appear on TV g_____ s_____ and win prizes.
6. A TV show that's intended to make people laugh is called a c_____.
7. A factual program that allows viewers to learn things is called a d_____.

28.2 Follow-up

According to the views discussed in the article in Reading 28.2, are the sentences below true or false?

1. The description in the 100-year-old text is true today.   T   F
2. People in different countries have similar tastes in music.   T   F
3. A characteristic of pop music is its wide range of instruments.   T   F
4. Lyrics are an important part of pop music's success.   T   F
5. Pop music was an early example of a global product.   T   F

28.3 Follow-up

Answer these questions about the article in Reading 28.3.

1. What's the most important requirement for a good movie?
2. For many movies, where does the story come from?
3. What should happen to the main character during a movie?
4. What does the screenwriter produce?
5. What's the name of the person who's responsible for making a movie?
6. Why are famous actors important for the commercial success of a movie?

American English	British English
movie	film
cinema/ movie theater	cinema

28

28.1 Language Summary — Talking about TV programs

Important things that have happened in the world are discussed in the `news`.
Big American `movies` are made in Hollywood.
My friend appeared on a TV `game show` and won some money.
Last night, I watched a `documentary` on TV about African elephants.
Did you watch that new `comedy` show last night? It was really funny.
TV programs whose stars are ordinary people are called `reality TV` shows.
Hundreds of famous people have been interviewed on the `talk show`.
The program's on every Thursday night. It's a `series` that's on for six weeks.
TV programs are `broadcast` in different ways: For example, there's `terrestrial` TV, `satellite` TV, `broadband` TV and `cable` TV.
There are different ways to `translate` a foreign language so that TV viewers can understand it. Sometimes written translations, called `subtitles`, are used. Sometimes, another speaker translates. In this case, we say the sound is `dubbed (over)`.

→ LANGUAGE PRACTICE 28.1 → PAGE 112

28.2 Language Summary — Talking about music

A person who sings is called a `singer`.
When several `musicians` play together, we say they're a `group` or a `band`.
The two broad categories of music are `pop music` and `classical music`.
When you buy just one song it's called a `single`. A collection of songs by the same singer or band is called an `album`.
The words of songs are called `lyrics`.

Examples of common musical `instruments`:
`guitar` `piano` `drum` `violin` `trumpet` `saxophone`

→ LANGUAGE PRACTICE 28.2 → PAGE 112

28.3 Language Summary — Talking about stories

`Fiction` is a general word for `stories` that are imaginary (not true stories).
The people in stories are called `characters`.
A `novel` is a book that tells a story.
A `writer` is a general name for someone who writes things – for example, stories.
`Actors` are people who `play parts`. They pretend to be characters.
When a `screenwriter` writes a movie, he or she produces a `script`.
A `director` guides actors and controls the making of a movie.
Computers are used to create `special effects` in movies – for example, flying spaceships.

→ LANGUAGE PRACTICE 28.3 → PAGE 112

Talking Point 28

Square Eyes

1

These days, if someone doesn't own a television set, you think they're slightly strange. In most developed countries, the percentage of homes with at least one TV is in the high nineties. In many countries, the figure is 99%.

If – as the statistics suggest – television is such an essential part of our lives, why do we criticize it so much? How often have you said or heard, "There's nothing but garbage on TV tonight", or similar – and then turned the television on anyway.

Then, occasionally, there are those fascinating programs that get everyone talking. The next morning, a friend or colleague will ask, "Did you watch … last night?" and a lively conversation follows.

2
Talk about the observations in **1**. How do they compare with the situation in your country and with your opinions about television programs?

3
What sorts of programs do you like to watch on TV? Talk about:
- the types of programs you like (for example, talk shows, documentaries …)
- specific programs you enjoyed, recently and in the past

What kinds of programs do you hate?

4
Talk about current television trends in your country. What kinds of programs are popular at the moment? How have TV programs changed in recent times?

UNIT 29
ENJOY YOUR STAY

29.1 Talking about tourist accommodations
29.2 Making accommodation arrangements
29.3 Discussing faults and problems

29.1 Reading

HOTEL ROOM 747

At Mojave Airport in California, there's an "airplane retirement home". If that sounds strange, it looks even stranger. Hundreds of out-of-use aircraft stand silently in the sand in the Mojave Desert with their silver bodies shining in the sun. It's like a scene from a science fiction movie. What's the connection between this surreal place and an article about hotels? The link is Swedish entrepreneur Oscar Dios who had the idea of buying a "retired" Boeing 747 and recycling it by turning it into a hostel. But where to locate it? Preferably, at a place where a plane can land and where there's a demand for overnight accommodation. The answer was obvious: at an airport.

The idea worked. Today, at Arlanda Airport in Stockholm, guests can stay at the Jumbo Hostel. The now static converted Jumbo Jet has 25 rooms and nine separate bathrooms. There's also a honeymoon suite – the only room with an **en-suite** bathroom – located in the aircraft's cockpit.

Clearly, the interior isn't as spacious as a conventional hotel. However, it has many familiar hotel features, mixed with a distinctive airline style. The rooms use the original overhead luggage compartments as wardrobes. There's a small lobby with a front desk, staffed by receptionists wearing retro airline uniforms. "Bed and breakfast" is also available thanks to a dining room where breakfast is served on small trays, in the style of an in-flight meal.

29.2 Reading

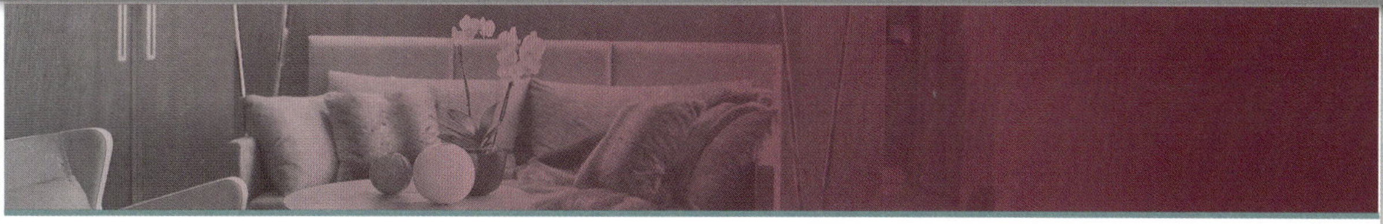

Reservations and payments – FAQ

HOME | SITEMAP | IMPRESSUM

- HOME
- ROOMS AND PRICES
- RESERVATIONS AND PAYMENTS – FAQ
- SITE MAP
- CONTACT

1. I received an email to confirm my reservation, giving a reservation number. I've printed out this confirmation. Is this the only document I'll need when I check in?

2. I paid a deposit when I booked my room. When do I have to pay the balance?

3. I paid for my room in advance. So why do I need to give my credit card number when I check in?

4. Breakfast is included in the price of my room. But what if I have other meals and drinks at the hotel restaurant/bar during my stay? Can these be added to my bill and paid when I check out?

5. The website says that there are no vacancies for the night I want to stay. If there's a cancelation and the hotel is no longer fully booked, could you notify me?

6. I've booked a standard room. When I check in, is it possible to upgrade to a larger one and pay the difference?

7. You offer reduced prices for advanced bookings. Are there special offers for last-minute reservations?

8. I've paid for my room in advance, but I need to cancel my booking. Can I get a refund?

29.3 Reading

Customer Care Training

HANDOUT Nº 1

Understanding the most common causes of complaints (queixas)

How can you, as a member of the hotel team, help to reduce the number of complaints from customers? The first step is to understand the different types of problems and faults that people complain about in hotels. These include six situations:

1. Something is **missing** from the room – e.g. there's no shower gel.
2. Something in the room is **dirty** – e.g. there's mud on the carpet.
3. Something is **damaged** – e.g. a coat hook has broken off the wall.
4. Something **doesn't work** or is **faulty** – e.g. there's something wrong with the TV.
5. Something is **unsafe** – e.g. a bare electric wire is sticking out from under the minibar. (fio desencapado)
6. Something is making the room **uncomfortable** – e.g. a cold draft is blowing into the room.

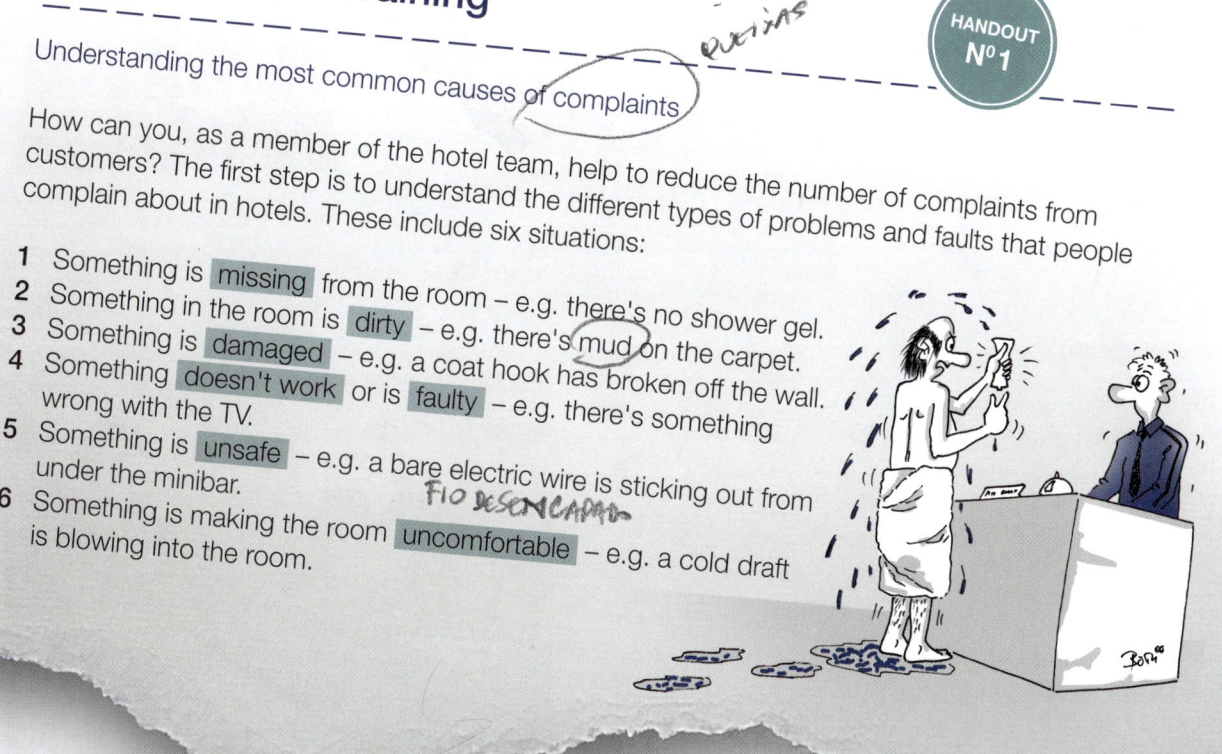

29.1 Listening (Track 47)

Part A You're going to hear three different people talking about where they stayed on a recent vacation. Listen and match each person's comments (1–3) to a place (A–C).

1. ___ A hotel
2. ___ B campground
3. ___ C guesthouse

Part B Look at the transcripts of the conversations on page 139. Find words that are associated with A, B and C above.

29.2 Listening (Track 48)

Part A You're going to hear a hotel receptionist speaking in four telephone conversations about accommodation arrangements. Listen to the subject of each conversation. For each one, mark one or both of the boxes.

Subject	dates/timing	payments/money
1	X	X
2	X	
3	X	X
4		X

Part B Now complete these sentences from the conversations.

1. We ask you for a 30% d _eposit_ today to confirm the booking.
2. Then, you pay the b _alance_ when you check out.
3. We've got no rooms free on the 18th – we're f _ully_ b _ooked_, I'm afraid.
4. We have a v _acancy_ on the 19th – I have a room free then.
5. So, because it's a last-minute cancelation, we can't give you a r _efund_.
6. That's our bed-and-breakfast rate, so obviously breakfast is i _ncluded_.

29.3 Listening (Track 49)

Part A You're going to hear a conversation at a hotel front desk. A customer is complaining about a problem with her room. Listen and mark one or more key words below which describe the problem.

Something is…
A damaged X
B faulty X
C missing ☐
D uncomfortable X

Part B Look at the transcript of the conversation on page 140. Find passages that match the key words you marked in Part A.

89

29.1 Follow-up

Answer these questions about the article in Reading 29.1.

1. What are the advantages of locating the Jumbo Hostel at an airport?

2. Do the rooms in the hostel have bathrooms?

3. Apart from the fact that the hostel is a plane, what other features give it an airline style?

29.2 Follow-up

The sentences below give answers to the Frequently Asked Questions (FAQ) in Reading 29.2. Match each answer to one of the questions (1–8).

A This is required to cover any extras you purchase.
B You should also bring some ID and a credit card.
C Yes, by registering your email address.
D Yes, provided a suitable room is available.
E This will need to be settled when you check out.
F Yes, but you must do this at least 48 hours ahead.
G Yes, you can settle these extras at the end of your stay.
H No. To get the best deal, reserve as far ahead as possible.

29.3 Follow-up

Use the words below to complete the sentences. Then look at Reading 29.3 to check your answers.

| damaged | dirty | faulty | missing | uncomfortable | unsafe |

1. Something is _____ from the room – e.g. there's no shower gel.
2. Something in the room is _____ – e.g. there's mud on the carpet.
3. Something is _____ – e.g. a coat hook has broken off the wall.
4. Something doesn't work or is _____ – e.g. there's something wrong with the TV.
5. Something is _____ – e.g. a bare electric wire is sticking out from under the minibar.
6. Something is making the room _____ – e.g. a cold draft is blowing into the room.

"I know it's small. That's why we call it a minibar."

29

29.1 Language Summary — Talking about tourist accommodations

Accommodations are places where tourists and business travelers can stay overnight.
Guesthouses or hostels are similar to hotels, but generally offer more basic services – for example, rooms may not have their own private bathrooms.
A campground is a place where you can pitch a tent and camp overnight.
When you're camping, you can heat up food on a small cooker called a stove.
Bed and breakfast means a room for the night and breakfast in the morning.
In a hotel, half-board accommodation includes breakfast and dinner in the evening.
With full-board accommodation, the price includes all meals at the hotel.
Customers staying in hotels are generally called guests.
The area just inside the entrance to a hotel is called the lobby.
The desk in a hotel lobby is called the front desk, or the reception.
A person who works at a front desk / reception is called a receptionist.
In hotels and homes, the room where people eat is called the dining room.

→ LANGUAGE PRACTICE 29.1 → PAGE 113

29.2 Language Summary — Making accommodation arrangements

If you make an online reservation, you generally receive an email to confirm it. This confirmation usually contains a number or code.
An advance(d) booking is a booking made quite a long time before a trip or stay.
Often, when you book in advance, you also have to pay in advance.
Sometimes when you make a booking, you pay a deposit. This means you pay a part of the price in advance. Then later, you pay the balance.
If a hotel has no rooms free, we say it has no vacancies. The hotel is fully booked.
When you cancel a booking you no longer want, it's sometimes possible to get your money back.
But it's not always possible to get a refund after a cancelation.
When you arrive at a hotel, you check in at the front desk. On leaving, you check out.

→ LANGUAGE PRACTICE 29.2 → PAGE 113

29.3 Language Summary — Discussing faults and problems

There's something wrong with the TV. It doesn't work properly. It's faulty.
I wasn't satisfied with my room, so I went to the front desk to complain.
They hadn't cleaned the room. It was dirty.
There was no remote control for the TV. It was missing.
The light switch wasn't completely broken, but it was damaged.
The broken switch was dangerous. It was certainly unsafe.
The bed was really hard. It was pretty uncomfortable.
There's a problem with the TV. It won't turn on.

→ LANGUAGE PRACTICE 29.3 → PAGE 113

Talking Point

Star Ratings

1
In the world of hotels, stars are precious. The more stars a hotel has, the more money it can charge its customers. Five stars is normally the top rating. Although there's a hotel in Dubai which gave itself seven stars.

There's no single organization, internationally, that awards numbers of stars to hotels. There are no standardized specifications that describe the facilities you should find in a one-, two-, three-, four- or five-star hotel. There is, however, a generally accepted view on how good a hotel with each star rating should be.

2
In your opinion, what are the main characteristics that differentiate better-quality hotels from lower-quality ones? What kinds of things define how good a hotel is? Write a list.

3
Using the ideas on your list, give some examples of the kinds of things you'd expect to find at a hotel with:
- ★ one star
- ★★★ three stars
- ★★★★★ five stars

Now compare your ideas with the descriptions on the *Resource Sheet*.

4
Luxury is not everyone's cup of tea. Talk about your idea of a great or interesting place to stay. It could be anything from a tent to a boat.

THE BIG PICTURE

30.1 Describing directions and movement
30.2 Explaining causes and effects
30.3 Discussing certain and uncertain information

30.1 Reading

Turn off the lights and look backward through time …

We've all looked up at the night sky and wondered about the mysteries of the universe. The moon and stars are incredibly beautiful. However, for most people, the true beauty of the night sky is partly hidden. That's because, if you live in a city, or even a reasonable distance away from one, your view of the stars is seriously reduced by "light pollution" from street lights shining into the sky.

It's only when you spend a night in a really wild, remote location that you can observe a true "big sky" – one where the only light you see is that shining down, out of space. These perfect conditions also offer the best chance to see a shooting star flying across the night sky. One of the amazing things about gazing into space is knowing that you're looking backward, through time. That's because the stars are so far away that the light coming from them has taken years to travel through space – for many stars, millions of years. Therefore, looking around the night sky gives a picture, not of the present, but of the past.

30.2 Reading

Meteors, meteorites and **meteoroids**: understanding **shooting stars**

Shooting stars are caused by meteoroids — small pieces of rock from space. As a result of the sun's gravity, **meteoroids** travel through space, orbiting the sun.

Frequently, meteoroids fly into the earth's atmosphere. Generally, they arrive at very high speed — traveling at tens of thousands of kilometers/miles per hour. Because of their high speed, the rocks compress (squash) the air in front of them with huge force. This force causes the air to heat up to an extremely high temperature, which causes the rock to heat up, too. Due to the heat, the meteoroid glows white hot as it flies across the sky. The heat makes the rock shine brightly and break up, leaving a white trail behind it — called a **meteor**. Many meteoroids burn up completely as a result of the heat. But some small rocks survive and fall to earth. Space rocks that hit the ground are called **meteorites**.

30.3 Reading

HOW MUCH DO WE REALLY KNOW ABOUT THE UNIVERSE?

It's said that travel broadens the mind. Generally, it's thought that knowledge of other countries is a sign of education and experience. However, this isn't true about knowledge of places beyond the earth. Most people know very little about space — especially the universe beyond the eight planets of our solar system. This is understandable, as the unimaginable size of space makes it difficult to know where to begin. What's more, even the experts are still guessing about many of the deep, dark secrets of the universe.

WHERE ARE WE IN SPACE?

Our star, the sun, is in a galaxy (a huge group of stars, planets, space rocks, dust and gas) called the Milky Way. It's not known exactly how many stars are in the Milky Way, but it's estimated that the number is between 200 billion and 400 billion. Apart from the sun, the closest star to us in the Milky Way is Proxima Centauri. This star is 4.2 light years away — that is, the distance traveled by light in 4.2 years. By comparison, light takes just over eight minutes to travel from the sun to the earth.

WHAT ABOUT OTHER GALAXIES OUTSIDE THE MILKY WAY?

The nearest galaxy outside the Milky Way is the Canis Major Dwarf Galaxy, 25,000 light years away. It's believed that it contains approximately one billion stars. In the "observable universe" — that is, parts of space where things can be seen or detected from earth — it's estimated that there are about 170 billion galaxies. It's thought that most galaxies contain between 100 billion and one trillion stars. Based on this, one recent, very rough estimate of the number of stars in the universe is 3,000,000,000,000,000,000,000,000.

30.1 Listening (Track 50)

Look at the explanation by Umberto Fabi, an astronomer. He describes how spaceships orbit the earth – and why astronauts are weightless. Complete the explanation using the words below. Then listen and check your answers.

around   away   downward   forward   into   off   through   toward   upward

"First, the spaceship's rockets lift it 1 _____ the ground and push it 2 _____, vertically. This takes it 3 _____ from the earth and, eventually, 4 _____ space. When the ship reaches space, it turns to become horizontal. Then its rockets push it until it reaches a very high speed. The ship's rockets then stop. Now, if the ship were still in the earth's atmosphere, it would slow down as it flew 5 _____ the air – due to air resistance. But because there's no air in space, the ship doesn't slow down when its rockets stop. It keeps moving 6 _____ at the same speed."

"Most people think that, above the earth, in space, there's no gravity. They think that's why astronauts are weightless. But that's not true. The earth's gravity continues to pull the spaceship and the astronauts 7 _____. However, because the ship is moving so fast, as it falls it doesn't move 8 _____ the earth. Instead, it travels 9 _____ the earth. So when a spaceship and its crew are in orbit, and weightless, they're actually constantly falling. And gravity is still pulling them."

30.2 Listening (Track 51)

Part A You're going to hear Umberto Fabi discussing the danger of large space rocks hitting earth, and explaining how they can be spotted in advance. Listen, then answer the questions below.

1. What are very big space rocks called?
2. What's an "extinction event"?
3. What size of space rock could cause an extinction event?
4. Where's the PS1 Observatory?
5. How does the PS1 Observatory spot large space rocks?

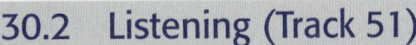

Part B Now complete these extracts from the interview with the words below.

because   cause   due   make   result

1. "… we believe it would _____ an extinction event …"
2. "So, _____ of this danger, there's a telescope …"
3. "But, _____ to all the stars in the sky, it's difficult to spot space rocks."
4. "So the stars _____ them difficult to see."
5. "And, as a _____ of that comparison, they can spot moving rocks."

30.3 Listening (Track 52)

You're going to hear four comments from a conversation by someone who read the article about the universe in Reading 30.3. Listen and compare the way the comments are said with the way they're written in the article.

30.1 Follow-up

The sentences below are based on the article in Reading 30.1. Use the words below to complete them.

~~across~~   around   ~~away~~   ~~into~~   out   ~~through~~   up

1 The light from the stars takes years to travel **THROUGH** space and reach earth.
2 Light pollution is light from cities that shines **UP**, **INTO** the sky at night.
3 You see light pollution even if you live quite a long distance **AWAY** from a city.
4 A big sky is when the only light is that coming **OUT** of space from the stars.
5 A shooting star is a light that travels **ACROSS** the night sky.
6 On clear nights, you can see thousands of stars when you look **AROUND** the sky.

30.2 Follow-up

Answer these questions about the article in Reading 30.2.

1 What causes shooting stars?

2 Why do meteoroids travel through space?

3 When a meteoroid flies into the earth's atmosphere, what happens to the air?

4 Why do meteoroids shine brightly?

5 In the end, what can happen to meteoroids?

30.3 Follow-up

Try to fill in the correct numbers without looking at Reading 30.3. Then look at the article and check your answers.

4.2   8   25,000   170 billion   400 billion   1 trillion   3 trillion, trillion

1 It's estimated that there are between 200 billion and _____ stars in our galaxy.
2 The closest star to earth, apart from the sun, is _____ light years away.
3 Light takes just over _____ minutes to travel from the sun to the earth.
4 The nearest galaxy outside the Milky Way is _____ light years away.
5 It's estimated that there are about _____ galaxies in the universe.
6 It's thought that most galaxies contain between 100 billion and _____ stars.
7 A very rough estimate of the number of stars in the universe is _____.

30.1 Language Summary — Describing directions and movement

walk `up` the stairs
run `down` the hill
go `into` a building
get `out of` the house
move `away from` the north, `to` the south
sail `across` the ocean
walk `around` the lake
drive `through` the tunnel

---

go `forward(s)` = →   go `backward(s)` = ←
go `upward(s)` = ↑   go `downward(s)` = ↓
go `toward(s)` something = →|

→ LANGUAGE PRACTICE 30.1 → PAGE 113

30.2 Language Summary — Explaining causes and effects

The delay to the flight was `caused by` bad weather.

The delay happened
▸ `as a result of` bad weather.
▸ `because of`
▸ `due to`

Bad weather can
▸ `make` flights late.
▸ `cause` flights `to` be late.

→ LANGUAGE PRACTICE 30.2 → PAGE 114

30.3 Language Summary — Discussing certain and uncertain information

`It's known that` there are billions of stars in the Milky Way.
`It's not known` exactly how many stars there are.

`It's said that` there may be life in the Solar System.
`It's thought that`

`It's believed that` there are 200 billion to 400 billion stars in the Milky Way.
`It's estimated that`

→ LANGUAGE PRACTICE 30.3 → PAGE 114

Talking Point

The BIG Debate

1
To most people, the idea of UFOs and aliens is absurd, or at best highly improbable. But what do the facts and numbers tell us? It's a fact that, in the universe, there are billions of stars, and many of them have planets orbiting them. This raises two interesting questions:
- What's the probability that earth is the only planet in the universe with life on it?
- What's the probability that there are millions of other planets with life on them?

Discuss your views on these questions. Give reasons for your opinions.

2
If probability suggests that the universe contains huge numbers of planets where life exists, it also raises another idea: that some of these planets might have very primitive creatures on them, and that others could be inhabited by creatures that are much more intelligent and advanced than humans. In the second case, what's the probability that some highly developed creatures in the universe have the technology to look or travel enormous distances across space – possibly in ways that we humans cannot understand? Then what are the chances that creatures like these have already noticed or visited the earth?

3
Imagine that, in the future, humans find a faraway planet that has life on it, and that we have the technology to travel the enormous distance to reach it. Should we go there? If so, what should the motives of our mission be, as "visiting aliens"? To make observations in secret? To introduce ourselves? To colonize the planet?

4
Think about the kinds of UFO sightings you've heard about. In your view, how credible are they? Compare them with your ideas about the motives of visiting aliens discussed in **3**, and how intelligent and advanced the visitors are likely to be.

Grammar Summary 26–30

Linking and contrasting

We can use the following words and phrases to link similar and contrasting points:
We use `too`, `as well` and `also` to signal that a point has a similar message to the last one.

First point	Second point
The meal was nice.	It was pretty cheap, `too`.
The meal was nice.	It was pretty cheap, `as well`.
The meal was nice.	It was `also` pretty cheap.

We use `either` to signal a similar message in `negative` sentences.

First point	Second point
The meal was nice.	It `wasn't` expensive, `either`.

We use `but`, `although` or `however` to signal that a point contrasts with the last one.

First point	Second point
The meal was nice,	`but` it was pretty expensive.
The meal was nice,	`although` it was pretty expensive.
The meal was nice.	`However`, it was pretty expensive.

Causes and effects

We can use the following language to give reasons why things happen.

Result		Reason
There were delays to flights	▶ `as a result of`	snow.
	▶ `because of`	
	▶ `due to`	

Reason		Result
The region was hit by snow.	▶ `As a result of`	the bad weather, flights were delayed.
	▶ `Because of`	
	▶ `Due to`	

Grammar Summary 26–30

Movement and direction

We can use the following words after verbs to describe movement and direction:

up = ↑	go up the stairs	
down = ↓	go down the stairs	
into = enter a space	go into the room	
out of = exit a space	go out of the room	
away from = increase distance	go away from the danger	
across = from one side to another	go across the road	
around = make a tour or detour	go around the obstacle	
through = in, then out of the other side	go through the door	

forward(s) = in the direction you're facing	go forward(s)
backward(s) = the opposite of forward(s)	go backward(s)
upward(s) = up	go upward(s)
downward(s) = down	go downward(s)

go toward(s) something = move closer   go toward(s) the destination

Certain and uncertain information

In formal English, we often use the passive to talk about shared knowledge that is certain or uncertain. To talk about knowledge, we can use verbs such as: think , say , know , believe and estimate .

Active	Historians think that the building is over 1,000 years old.
Passive	It is thought that the building is over 1,000 years old.
Active	Researchers estimate that the country's population is growing by 2% per year.
Passive	It is estimated that the country's population is growing by 2% per year.
Active	Nobody knows how quickly the earth's atmosphere is warming.
Passive	It is not known how quickly the earth's atmosphere is warming.

100

Vocabulary Summary 26–30

Money language

bank account	to lend	mortgage	debts
savings	loan	to repay	to owe
to borrow	interest	to withdraw	

Positive feelings

brilliant	glad	satisfying	funny
fantastic	pleased	proud	amused
awesome	satisfied	fun	amusing

Negative feelings

terrified	disappointed	miserable	embarrassed
terrifying	disappointing	angry	embarrassing
frightened	terrible	annoyed	depressed
frightening	awful	annoying	depressing

TV programs

news	reality TV (show)	satellite TV	subtitles
movie	talk show	cable TV	dubbed
game show	drama	terrestrial TV	
documentary	series	broadband TV	
comedy	broadcast	digital TV	

Music

group	classical music	guitar	banjo
band	single	drum	recorder
singer	album	piano	trombone
musician	track	violin	bagpipes
song	instrument	trumpet	accordion
pop music	lyrics	saxophone	

Stories

fiction	movie	actor/actress	special effects
character	screenwriter	part	
novel	script	director	

Accommodations

to pitch (a tent)	en-suite room	advance(d) booking	cancel
stove	lobby	to pay a deposit	cancelation
bed and breakfast	front desk	to pay the balance	refund
half-board	receptionist	fully booked	check in
full-board	to confirm	included	check out
guest	confirmation	no vacancies	bill
hostel	book in advance	upgrade	

Skills Summary 26–30

After Units 26 to 30, you can ...

Skill	Section
▶ discuss everyday financial issues	26.1
▶ refer to past transactions	26.2
▶ refer to past situations in markets	26.2
▶ say large numbers precisely	26.3
▶ say large numbers approximately	26.3
▶ say decimals	26.3
▶ say percentages	26.3
▶ describe positive feelings	27.1
▶ describe negative feelings	27.2
▶ connect complementary ideas	27.3
▶ connect contrasting ideas	27.3
▶ describe consequences	27.3
▶ refer to types of TV programs	28.1
▶ refer to TV broadcast types	28.1
▶ discuss types of music	28.2
▶ refer to common musical instruments	28.2
▶ discuss issues relating to stories	28.3
▶ discuss issues relating to movies	28.3
▶ understand and discuss details of accommodations	29.1
▶ enquire about accommodations	29.2
▶ book accommodations	29.2
▶ describe faults	29.3
▶ describe how things move	30.1
▶ refer to causes	30.2
▶ refer to resulting effects	30.2
▶ refer to certain information	30.3
▶ refer to unknown information	30.3
▶ refer to estimates	30.3

Language Practice

Unit 16

Language Practice 16.1

Rewrite each opinion using a phrase that means the same as the one on the left.

1. I think it's true.   In _____, it's true.
2. I believe that's possible.   I'd _____ that's possible.
3. I know it'll be difficult.   I'm _____ it'll be difficult.
4. I don't know if we can do that.   I'm _____ if we can do that.
5. That's my opinion.   That's my point _____.
6. That's also a good idea.   That's a good idea, _____.

Language Practice 16.2

Use the phrases below to complete the table.

I agree.   I don't really agree.   I disagree.   I'm not sure I agree.   I totally agree.
I totally disagree.

strong agreement
1 _____
2 _____
3 _____
4 _____
5 _____
strong disagreement 6 _____

Language Practice 16.3

Complete the sentences to report the comments. Use the same style as the example.

1. "I have an appointment in the morning."   She said *she had an appointment in the morning* .
2. "I like the idea."   She said _____.
3. "I'm busy at the moment."   She said _____.
4. "I'm thinking about the idea."   She said _____.
5. "I can come to the party."   She said _____.
6. "I'll phone soon."   She said _____.

Unit 17

Language Practice 17.1

Use one word to complete each of the sentences about telephoning.

1. Excuse me. I just need to _____ a phone call.
2. I'll call you on the train, from my _____ phone.
3. I'll contact you in a couple of days. I'll _____ you a call on Thursday or Friday.
4. An indoor phone that has a wireless handset is called a _____ phone.
5. How do you get the numbers to show on the screen, so you can _____ a phone number?
6. Press the button with the red phone symbol on it to _____ up and end the call.
7. What's that noise? Is someone's phone _____?

Language Practice

Language Practice 17.2

Complete the telephone conversation.

- Hello.
- Hello. 1 _____ I 2 _____ to Carla, please?
- Just a 3 _____ . I'll 4 _____ you to her office.
- Thanks.
- Sorry. I'm afraid she's on the phone. Her line's 5 _____ .
- Oh, right.
- Would you like to 6 _____ ?
- No, it's OK. I'll 7 _____ her 8 _____ later.

Language Practice 17.3

Complete the sentences to report the questions.

1. Where's the restaurant?   He asked _____.
2. Is the store open?   He asked _____.
3. When does the store close?   He asked _____.
4. How does the machine work?   He asked _____.
5. Does the room have a phone?   He asked _____.

Unit 18

Language Practice 18.1

Write the words below next to the matching descriptions in 1–8.

automatic | button | cable | electricity | plug | remote control | socket | volume

1. a source of power for many appliances _____
2. allows you to control a TV from a distance _____
3. a point of connection to the electricity supply, in a wall _____
4. the level of sound, of a TV for example _____
5. something you press to control a device _____
6. the connecter that goes into an electrical socket _____
7. the long wire used to connect an appliance _____
8. not manual – controls itself _____

Language Practice 18.2

Complete the instructions on the right so that they mean the same as those on the left. Use the words below.

in | in | off | on | out | plug | put | take | turn | turn | turn | unplug | up

1. Increase the level of the sound.   =   _____ _____ the volume.
2. Connect the device to an electrical socket.   =   _____ _____ the device.
3. Press the button to start the appliance.   =   _____ _____ the appliance.
4. Insert the battery.   =   _____ _____ the battery.
5. Remove the battery.   =   _____ _____ the battery.
6. Press the button to stop the appliance.   =   _____ _____ the appliance.
7. Disconnect the device.   =   _____ the device.

Language Practice

Language Practice 18.3

Rewrite each sentence to include the word in parentheses in the correct place. Each time, write two possible answers.

1 I'll plug the TV. *(in)*
   _____ / _____

2 Turn the light. *(on)*
   _____ / _____

3 Could you turn the volume, please? *(down)*
   _____ / _____

4 How do you take the battery? *(out)*
   _____ / _____

Unit 19

Language Practice 19.1

Fill in the missing words to complete the sentences below.

1 There's no need to do the dishes by hand. Just put everything in the *d*_____.
2 Before you put the pizza in to bake, you need to preheat the *o*_____.
3 It takes less than five minutes to cook a small potato in a *m*_____.
4 It's easy to clean a tiled floor. But it's harder to clean a *c*_____.
5 On a hot day, you can close the *d*_____ to stop the sun shining through the windows.
6 As soon as you've finished pouring the milk, put it back in the *f*_____.
7 I like your wall covering. Where did you get the *w*_____?
8 I hate decorating. The most boring job is *p*_____.

Language Practice 19.2

Fill in the missing words.

1 The walls of the house are built from clay *b*_____.
2 The house is made of rock. It's built from *s*_____.
3 *C*_____ is made from cement, sand and gravel.
4 What sort of trees does the *w*_____ come from?
5 The *g*_____ in the window is broken.
6 The cat climbed up onto the *r*_____ of the building.
7 The lawn needs mowing. The *g*_____ is getting long.

Language Practice 19.3

Match the pairs of opposite words for describing designs.

bright 1   A light
dark 2   B ugly
beautiful 3   C original
modern 4   D dull
common 5   E old-fashioned

105

Unit 20

Language Practice 20.1

Use suitable words to complete the sentences about jobs around the home.

1. Before we do anything else, we need to _____ _____ this mess.
2. How can I vacuum the house? The _____ _____ has broken down.
3. I was going to _____ the grass, but the lawn mower has run out of gas.
4. Do you have a broom I can use to _____ the floor?
5. All this stuff is garbage. I'm going to _____ it _____.
6. Watch the iron. It's hot. I've just _____ these clothes.

Language Practice 20.2

Complete 1–6 using the correct forms of the words.

1. I'll finish the job _____ (easy) by the end of the week.
2. We'll have to walk _____ (fast) to get there on time.
3. You'll get there _____ (+ quick) if you take the other route.
4. I can't work _____ (+ hard) than I'm working at the moment.
5. The whole team did a good job. They played _____ (good).
6. This new design is an improvement. It works _____ (+ good).

Language Practice 20.3

Change the sentences. Use the past with use(d) to.

1. At school, I was good at art.
2. I lived in that town in the late 1990s.
3. As a teenager, I didn't like sports.
4. Where did you live during your studies?
5. In my first job, I never worked overtime.

Unit 21

Language Practice 21.1

Use alternative words, with the same meaning, to complete the second sentences about problems.

1. The *problem* is the weather's getting worse.
   The t *HINGs* is the weather's getting worse.
2. It's *difficult* to see what's going to happen.
   It's h *ARD* to see what's going to happen.
3. It *isn't possible* to get a flight.
   It's i *MPOSSIBLE* to get a flight.
4. I *can't* travel today.
   I w *ill* b *e* a *BLE* t *O* travel tomorrow.

Language Practice

Language Practice 21.2

Look at the suggestion below. Rephrase it different ways, starting with the words in 1–6.

Would you like to go for a coffee?

1 Shall _____?
2 Let _____.
3 Why _____?
4 What _____?
5 We _____.
6 How _____?

Language Practice 21.3

Rewrite the sentences on the left in the past, using able to or manage to.

Present	Past	
1 I can finish the job.	I was able to finish the job.	(able to)
2 We can get some tickets.		(able to)
3 I can't answer all the questions.		(able to)
4 They can't find a hotel.		(able to)
5 I can solve the problem.		(manage to)
6 We can't get there on time.		(manage to)

Unit 22

Language Practice 22.1

Match the specific social issues in 1–8 to the general social issues in A–H.

There's a shortage of two-bedroom apartments in the city. 1	A	education
It's always very wet at this time of year, so floods are a problem. 2	B	health
The cost of studying for a degree has risen steadily in recent years. 3	C	crime
The new sports center will contain a wide range of sports facilities. 4	D	real estate
If the hospital closes, local patients will have to travel over 80 miles. 5	E	economy
Over 90% of the residents said they could smell smoke from the plant. 6	F	climate
If the plant closes, local unemployment could reach 15%. 7	G	pollution
The bank has been robbed four times in the last three years. 8	H	recreation

Language Practice 22.2

Complete 1–6 using the correct combination of some, any, no and thing, body or where.

1 Does _____ know what time it is?
2 I put my keys down _____ and I can't find them.
3 I need to go shopping urgently. There's _____ in the fridge.
4 There was _____ waiting at the bus stop, so the bus didn't stop.
5 I'm just going out to get _____ to eat.
6 This is an amazing city. I've never been _____ like it.

107

Language Practice

Language Practice 22.3

Fill in the missing words.

1 The automotive m_____ is full of old cars.
2 There are several famous paintings in the art g_____.
3 This is a stone s_____ of the explorer.
4 A new show starts next week at the t_____.
5 The band are playing their first c_____ for almost five years.
6 The football game will be played at the brand-new s_____.
7 Do you know a good cafe or b_____ where we can go for a drink?
8 Let's go and buy a t_____ to eat at home.

Unit 23

Language Practice 23.1

Complete the conversations using suitable polite expressions.

1 _____. Could you tell me how to get to the Park Hotel?
2 Here's your cup of tea. – _____.
3 This is for you. It's heavy. It's solid gold. – Wow! _____.
4 _____? I didn't hear what you just said.
5 I was supposed to be here 20 minutes ago. _____.
6 Did I just stand on your foot? Sorry. – _____.
7 Here's your room key. – Thanks. – _____.

Language Practice 23.2

Rephrase the direct questions below in an indirect way to make them more polite.

1 Where does the airport shuttle leave from?
   Do you know _____?

2 Is there a bank close to here?
   Can you tell me _____?

3 Is it possible to have some food?
   I wonder _____?

4 Could I use the phone?
   I just wanted to ask _____?

Language Practice

Language Practice 23.3

Match the sentences in 1–10 to the characteristics in A–J. Then compare your answers with Language Summary 23.3.

She's not much fun to be with. She's	1	A	reliable.
She doesn't enjoy meeting new people. She's	2	B	shy.
She doesn't talk much. She's	3	C	serious.
She's easy to get to know and get along with. She's	4	D	funny.
She always does what she promises to do. She's	5	E	boring.
She makes us laugh. She's	6	F	lazy.
She doesn't get stressed. She's	7	G	quiet.
She doesn't have much of a sense of humor. She's	8	H	relaxed.
She doesn't like working. She's	9	I	hard-working.
She works hard. She's	10	J	friendly.

Unit 24

Language Practice 24.1

Match the pairs to make common phrases related to food and restaurants.

reserve a	1 D	A	bar
main	2 C	B	meal
service is	3 G	C	course
exclusive	4 E	D	table
snack	5 A	E	restaurant
fast	6 H	F	service
self-	7 F	G	included
three-course	8 B	H	food

Language Practice 24.2

Use suitable words to complete the comments made in a restaurant.

1 This is a local dish. I'm not sure how to ~~MARISCO~~ SAY it in English.
2 This is a KIND of shellfish. But I'm not sure what the name of it is in English.
3 I'm a VEGETARIAN I don't eat meat.
4 There's no alcohol in that. It's a SOFT drink.
5 What's in this? – Carrots, potatoes, broccoli and a few other VEGETABLES
6 There are three sorts of FRUITS in the pie: apples, pears and blackberries.

Language Practice 24.3

Make polite sentences using the words below and other necessary words.

1 could / me / the water / please / ?   COULD YOU PASS ME THE WATER PLEASE
2 would / anybody / some more vegetables / ?   WOULD ANYBODY BRING US SOME VEGETABLES
3 would / possible / some olive oil / please / ?   WOULD POSSIBLE BRING SOME OLIVE OIL PLEASE
4 would / mind / pass / me / the salt / please / ?   WOULD YOU MIND PASS ME THE SALT, PLEASE

Unit 25

Language Practice 25.1

Match the pairs to make common advertising phrases.

TV 1 **F** A price
50% 2 **C** B gift
free 3 **B** C off
half- 4 **A** D offer
book 5 **E** E now
special 6 **D** F commercial

Language Practice 25.2

Use suitable words to complete the sentences about precautions.

1 **BE** careful. That knife's sharp!
2 **MAKE** sure you lock the door when you go out.
3 In dry weather, it's **DANGEROUS** **TO** light fires in forests, as there's a risk of wild fires.
4 **TAKE** care. Have a safe trip.
5 It's important **NOT** **TO** waste electricity.

Language Practice 25.3

Use the words below to complete 1 and 3 in the table. Then write the correct forms of the words to complete 2 and 4.

decrease   drop   grow   increase   reduce   rise

↑ 1	to	GROW	to INCREASE	to	RISE
2	the		the	the	
↓ 3	to	DROP	to DECREASE	to	REDUCE
4	the		the	the	REDUCTION

Unit 26

Language Practice 26.1

Use the words below to complete the sentences about money.

account   borrow   interest   lend   owe   repay

1 I didn't have enough money to buy a new car, so I had to _____ some from the bank.
2 I asked for a loan, but the bank refused to _____ me any money.
3 I got a $20,000 loan. And the _____ rate was 4.2%.
4 I use the Internet to check how much money is on my bank _____.
5 It's going to take me 15 years to _____ the mortgage.
6 He told me he has no debts. He doesn't _____ any money.

Language Practice

Language Practice 26.2

Use suitable words in their past form to complete 1–8.

1 Why have I received a reminder? I _____ the bill last month.
2 He didn't get a loan from the bank. His parents _____ him the money.
3 I've just got a new car. I _____ it last week.
4 It was a fantastic vacation, but it was expensive. It _____ nearly $8,000.
5 I bought the stocks just before the market crashed, so I _____ a lot of money.
6 It was a short shopping trip because I ran out of cash. I _____ everything in two hours.
7 My house was for sale for over a year, then I eventually _____ it.
8 A friend of mine _____ €1.2 million in the lottery.

Language Practice 26.3

Write the numbers in words.

1 456,000
2 2,920,000
3 8,000,000,000
4 7.34
5 2,000,000,000,000

Unit 27

Language Practice 27.1

Use suitable words to complete the sentences about feelings.

1 I really enjoyed that. It was *f* _____ .
2 That was a great experience. I'm *g* _____ I did it.
3 I got a fairly good mark in the exam, so I'm quite *p* _____ .
4 The show was such a laugh – really *f* _____ .
5 I've got some *b* _____ news. We've won the first prize!

Language Practice 27.2

Complete the words to describe negative feelings, then compare your answers with Language Summary 27.2.

1 It wasn't as good as I hoped.	= I was *d* _____ .	It was *d* _____ .
2 I was angry.	= I was *a* _____ .	It was *a* _____ .
3 I was miserable.	= I was *d* _____ .	It was *d* _____ .
4 I was ashamed.	= I was *e* _____ .	It was *e* _____ .
5 It was really bad.	= It was *t* _____ .	It was *a* _____ .

Language Practice

Language Practice 27.3

Underline the correct word in each sentence below.

1 I enjoyed doing the job. I was well-paid, either/too.
2 All the stores were closed. Because/So we couldn't do any shopping.
3 There's lots of information on the website. The site's easy to navigate, as well / however.
4 It was an expensive meal. Also/However, it was worth the money.
5 I didn't bring any water with me. And I had no money to buy a drink, as well / either.

Unit 28

Language Practice 28.1

Match the categories of TV program below to the descriptions of specific programs in 1–6.

comedy show   documentary   drama series   game show   movie   talk show

1 Tell me more — Host Jim McDonald chats to a selection of celebrity guests.
2 Explorer — A look at the fascinating fish in the depths of the Pacific Ocean.
3 The Big Bonus — Can any of tonight's contestants win the $1,000,000 jackpot?
4 The Lighthouse — Episode 6. New hope of rescue for the shipwrecked crew.
5 Funny Fred — More laughs with Fred Farina.
6 Black Diamonds — A gang of bank robbers fall into a deadly trap.

Language Practice 28.2

Complete the words about music, on the right, to match the descriptions on the left.

1 a person who makes music — a m
2 a person who sings — a s
3 several people who play music together — a g   or a b
4 a recording of one song — a s
5 a recording of a collection of songs — an a
6 the words of a song — the l
7 a musical instrument with strings — a g
8 a musical instrument with keys — a p
9 a musical instrument you hit with sticks — a d

Language Practice 28.3

Match the comments in 1–5 to the most suitable words in A–E.

It's a really long book. It's over 600 pages. 1   A special effects
It's not a true story. 2   B script
I thought he played the part really well. 3   C novel
The walking dinosaurs looked very realistic. 4   D fiction
The conversations between the characters weren't very realistic. 5   E actor

112

Language Practice

Unit 29

Language Practice 29.1

Complete the sentences below about accommodations.

1. Is there a campground near here, or anywhere else we can p____ a tent?
2. I went into the hotel, but there was no receptionist at the f____ d____.
3. The room and the cost of all meals are included in the price – it's f____ - b____.
4. Excuse me. I'm going for breakfast. I'm looking for the d____ room.
5. The hotel was really busy. There were lots of other g____ staying there.
6. Shall we meet just inside the hotel entrance? At 6:00 p.m. in the l____?

Language Practice 29.2

Complete the terms on the right to match the descriptions on the left.

1. a reservation made on the Internet — an o____ b____
2. a message to say that a reservation is OK — a b____ c____
3. a part-payment made in advance — a d____
4. the final payment due, less an earlier part-payment — the b____
5. a notice to say that a hotel is fully booked — N____ v____
6. what you do when you leave a hotel at the end of your stay — c____ o____
7. when you get money back after canceling a purchase — a r____

Language Practice 29.3

Look at 1–5 and complete the words that describe faults and problems.

1. not clean — d____
2. lost / not there — m____
3. partly broken — d____
4. dangerous — u____
5. not comfortable — u____

Unit 30

Language Practice 30.1

Use the words below, which describe positions and directions, to complete the sentences.

across   around   away   down   into   out   through   up

1. It took me ages to walk ____ the stairs, all the way to the top floor.
2. When we walked ____ of the building, we all got wet in the pouring rain.
3. The station's on the other side of the street. We'll have to go ____ the road.
4. I walked ____ the outside of the car to check that it wasn't damaged.
5. They say that if a bear comes toward you, you shouldn't try to run ____ from it.
6. The ball rolled ____ the hill, all the way to the bottom.
7. When I walked ____ the room, everyone went silent.
8. There was a gust of wind, and the papers flew off the desk and went ____ the window.

Language Practice

Language Practice 30.2

Complete the sentences about causes and effects.

1 The highway was closed / because / snow.

2 Many people lost money / result / the stock market crash.

3 The breakdown was / cause / dirt in the car's gas tank.

4 There were traffic jams / due / roadwork.

5 The virus caused / the computer / crash.

Language Practice 30.3

Rewrite the sentences.

1 They estimate that there are billions of galaxies.
   It's

2 They think that there are over 200 billion stars in the Milky Way.
   It's

3 They don't know how big the universe is.
   It's

Extra Practice Unit 16

Part A Look at these two photos of people disagreeing. What message do they give about the different ways people say they disagree?

"I disagree."

"I disagree."

Part B Look at the descriptions about disagreeing by three people from three different cultures. Complete the missing words.

A "People are not afraid to say that they disagree with one another in my culture. But I don't think it's true that they express **1 d_____** directly. In most cases, they are reasonably tactful about it. Disagreeing is fine, as long as it's done in a friendly way."

B "Here, people find it difficult to say they disagree, even if it's done in a polite way. In fact, sometimes, people are so careful about what they say that you're not **2 s_____** whether they **3 a_____** or disagree with you."

C "I'd **4 s_____** that people in this country are direct when they disagree, and that doesn't really make anyone feel bad. People simply say what they think. That makes it easy to have discussions about points of **5 v_____**."

Part C Now put A–C in order, from the most direct to the least direct.

most direct → → least direct

Part D Match 1–5 below to one of the descriptions in A–C.

1 The way that people say they disagree is sometimes confusing.
2 Telling people that you don't agree with their views or ideas is simple.
3 There's no need to be particularly polite when you disagree.
4 There's no problem with saying you disagree if you do it politely.
5 People try to avoid disagreeing with others because they find it difficult.

Part E Which of the descriptions in A–C in Part B is most similar to how people disagree in your culture? Compare your answer with those from other people in the group in the next session.

Extra Practice Unit 17

Part A Use each of the words below once to complete the first two paragraphs of the article.

answer   back   busy   call   cell   cordless   make   message   ring   text

TELEPHONING: *TECHNOLOGY* VERSUS *CULTURE*

As telecommunications technology has advanced, telephones have changed massively. People no longer walk around town carrying **1** _____ phones as heavy as bricks. Inside homes, traditional telephones with curly wires have been replaced by **2** _____ phones that can be carried from room to room. And these days, phones don't just **3** _____ – they can play more or less any sound or music imaginable. It's not just phones themselves that have changed. As telephone technology has evolved, so has the way people **4** _____ phone calls. These days, if you want to exchange some simple information with someone, you might not phone them at all and instead just send a **5** _____ message. If you **6** _____ someone's cell phone and they don't **7** _____, or the line's **8** _____, you can leave a **9** _____ on their voicemail – even if it's just to say, "Can you phone me **10** _____?" – and be sure they'll get it as soon as they look at their phone. However, it's wrong to believe there's some kind of standard, modern phoning culture. Telephone technology has changed so much in recent decades that different age groups have developed very different phoning habits. This is especially true when it comes to owning and using cell phones.

Part B Find words or pairs of words in the completed article to match the descriptions below.

1 a telephone, for use inside a home, that has no wire
2 the sound made by a phone when someone calls
3 a written message sent to a cell phone
4 a word to say that someone's phone line is currently in use
5 a system for recording spoken messages by phone

Part C Read the last paragraph of the article. What are your opinions on the question of how people in different age groups use cell phones? Make notes and prepare to discuss the subject in the next session. You could use the language below to help you.

Generally, people in their twenties/thirties/forties/fifties/sixties/seventies…
sometimes/often/seldom…   make/use/send…   calls / text messages / …

116

Extra Practice Unit 18

Part A Use the words below to complete the article.

battery   button   charge   electricity   plug   remove   replace   socket

E-BIKES: BICYCLES WITH A BOOST

It's easy to understand why electric bicycles – or e-bikes – are growing in popularity. Pressing a **1** _____ in order to go up a hill is a lot easier than pedaling. What's more, the **2** _____ used to help power most electric bikes is free. Energy is collected when the bicycle goes downhill, or when the rider uses the brakes, and is used to **3** _____ a **4** _____. The energy is then stored and used later to help the rider go uphill – although e-bikes still need pedals. With some models, it's possible to get power from an external source. You simply connect a battery charger to the bike and **5** _____ it into a **6** _____ in the wall. However, since batteries are heavy, it's more efficient to have a small unit that's charged by the bike itself.

One e-bike system, called the Copenhagen Wheel, is simply a bicycle wheel with all its parts and battery contained inside the wheel. The advantage of the system, which was developed by a team from the Massachusetts Institute of Technology (MIT), is that it can be used on an ordinary bike. You simply **7** _____ the back wheel from your bicycle, **8** _____ it with a Copenhagen Wheel, and you have an instant e-bike.

Part B Are these sentences about e-bikes true or false?

1. More and more people are buying e-bikes.   T   F
2. E-bikes have batteries instead of pedals.   T   F
3. An e-bike's battery is charged as it goes uphill.   T   F
4. The brakes on e-bikes work by taking power from the battery.   T   F
5. The Copenhagen Wheel has a battery in it.   T   F
6. Copenhagen Wheels are only found on specially made e-bikes.   T   F

Part C Use each of the words below once to complete the description of the Copenhagen Wheel.

in   off   on   to

To fit a Copenhagen Wheel to an ordinary bike, simply take **1** _____ the old back wheel and put **2** _____ the Copenhagen Wheel. There's no need to connect cables **3** _____ the wheel or plug **4** _____ the battery to charge it. The wheel is a totally self-contained unit.

Part D In your opinion, what are some of the different reasons why people buy e-bikes? Write one or two paragraphs giving some examples. You could use the language below.

I think a common reason for buying an e-bike is if you …
Another possible reason is if you …

Extra Practice Unit 19

Part A Use each of the words below once to complete the article.

bright   dark   roof   simple   steel   window

How to make a SOLAR LIGHT from a plastic bottle

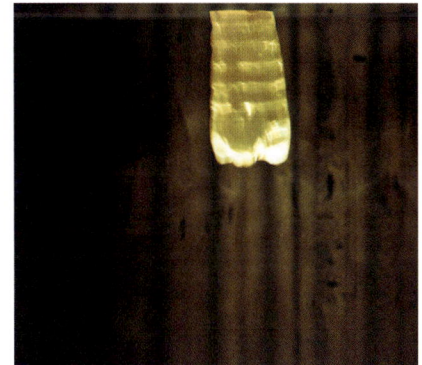

Solar bottle lights are cheap and **1**_____ to make, but are a very effective way to provide light inside buildings that have no **2**_____s – for instance, in barns or in the self-built homes that are common in many poorer countries. Inside these kinds of buildings it's always **3**_____, so very often, electric bulbs are used to provide light when it's needed during the day.

Bottle lights can be fitted easily to any building that's covered with a thin material – for example, **4**_____ sheets. To make one, fill a clear plastic bottle with water. Add a little bleach, to stop green bacteria from growing in the water, and put the cap on. Then, make a hole in the **5**_____ of the building that's the same diameter as the bottle. Put the bottle halfway through the hole so that the top half is outside in the sun and the bottom half is inside the building. Finally, seal around the hole with some waterproof tape, in order to fix the bottle and to stop rainwater from getting into the building. And the job's done.

The result is surprising. Inside the building, sunlight comes through the water so that the bottle produces a **6**_____ light. The light shines in all directions, just like an electric light bulb. The only difference is, instead of consuming electricity, the light uses free sunshine.

Part B According to the article, what four things are needed to make a solar bottle light?

a _____ + some _____ + some _____ + some _____

Part C Change one word in each of the sentences below to make them correct.

1 Most buildings have doors that are designed to let in daylight during the day. _____
2 Electric lights are not as dark as sunlight. _____
3 Solar bottle lights are normally put in the walls of buildings. _____
4 Concrete is a metal that can be used to make extremely thin sheets for roofs. _____
5 Most solar bottle lights are made from glass bottles. _____

Part D Look at the quotation below, from an architect. Why do you think sunlight is so important in the design of buildings? Think of some reasons, make notes and prepare to discuss the subject in the next session.

"One of the most important things in the design of a building – in both hot climates and cold climates – is how sunlight gets into the building, and how much sunlight gets into the building."

Extra Practice Unit 20

Part A Complete the article. Use the correct forms of the words in parentheses and, if necessary, add other words.

HOW FAIR IS INTERNATIONAL COMPETITION?

Today, almost every job, every company and every industry is feeling the pressure of competition from abroad. The chances are, there are workers in other countries who are trying to do 1 _____ (+ good) than you, in some way. Perhaps they're making things 2 _____ (+ cheap). Maybe they're trying to work 3 _____ (+ clever) to produce better goods or services. Possibly, they're trying to act 4 _____ (+ quick) in order to be the first to make the most of new opportunities.

«Are you sure this guy from Alaska is in a speed suit?»

Competition from abroad is a big subject. What's more, it's not just about who can work 5 _____ (+ hard) or 6 _____ (+ fast) than the rest. There's also the issue of whether some companies are competing 7 _____ (− fair) than those in other countries. For instance, if foreign competitors are making cheaper goods in their plant, is it because they're working 8 _____ (− safe) and putting their workers at risk?

Part B Use the correct form of each of the words below to complete the opinions about competition at work.

bad   dangerous   fast   good   hard

1 "In a lot of jobs, rushing results in people taking risks and working _____."
2 "Some people react _____ to pressure from competition – it improves their performance."
3 "Other people react _____ to pressure – it has a negative effect on their performance."
4 "If you're in a hurry, trying to work as _____ as possible, you can't possibly do a good job."
5 "Competition is the most effective way to push people to work _____."

Part C Do you agree or disagree with each of the opinions in Part B? Why? Make notes about your views below and prepare to discuss them in the next session.

1
2
3
4
5

Extra Practice Unit 21

Part A Fill in the missing words to complete the emails in A–E below. Note that the emails are not in the correct sequence.

A I've spoken to my team about the idea of meeting in Manila, and four of them could make it in the next four weeks. However, two team members won't be able to make it next month. The **1 t**_____ is, it's **2 h**_____ to find a time when everyone is available. Because it'll take three days to fly to Manila, have the meeting and come back. I guess we **3 c**_____ have a meeting without everyone there? What do you think? Sorry about these complications.

B That sounds like a good **4 i**_____. The important thing is that everyone can join the discussion. If you let me know a suitable date for you, I'll arrange things with my team.

C It was good to talk to you on Wednesday. As discussed, it would be great to have a project team meeting at your offices in Manila sometime next month. Unfortunately, I didn't **5 m**_____ to talk to all my colleagues about the idea yesterday. As always, it's **6 d**_____ to catch everyone together! But I'll speak to my team after the weekend and contact you at the beginning of next week.

D That **7 s**_____ good. Look forward to hearing from you then.

E Don't worry. I fully understand the problem. Of course, it's better to have a discussion where everyone can take part. Instead of holding a face-to-face meeting, **8 h**_____ about having a video conference? I know talking via webcam is not as good as actually meeting, but at least we could get everyone together that way. So **9 w**_____ about doing that instead?

Part B Now put the five emails in the correct sequence.

_____ → _____ → _____ → _____ → _____

Part C Find sentences in the emails to match these communication objectives. Write them below.

Explaining a problem
1 _____
2 _____
3 _____

Making a suggestion
4 _____
5 _____
6 _____

Accepting a suggestion
7 _____
8 _____

120

Extra Practice Unit 22

Part A The newspaper clippings below are from four different articles. There are three texts from each article. Put them in the correct groups.

Article 1   ☐-☐-☐   Article 3   ☐-☐-☐

Article 2   ☐-☐-☐   Article 4   ☐-☐-☐

A The latest crime figures are certainly worrying.

B The rate of unemployment hasn't fallen significantly.

C Are the government's new health plans working?

D There's been a significant rise in the amount of violence among young people.

E Several key forecasts are predicting the economy could enter a recession.

F Growing numbers of patients are complaining about the problem.

G What do students think about the situation?

H The cost of drugs is too high for many people.

I One question is whether jails can cope.

J More people could be out of work by the end of the year.

K In some areas, it has become difficult to find a place in college.

L Will the new plans allow more young people to remain in education longer?

Part B For each group, choose a word from one of the texts that sums up the subject of the article.

Group 1
Group 2
Group 3
Group 4

Part C Now find words in the texts in Part A to fill in the gaps below. Also underline the correct word:

something , somebody or somewhere .

1 A _____ is something / somebody / somewhere who's studying.
2 A _____ is something / somebody / somewhere that people go to study.
3 A _____ is something / somebody / somewhere that prisoners are sent to.
4 _____ are something / somebody / somewhere that people take when they're sick.
5 To be _____ means that something / somebody / somewhere is out of work.

Part D Think of a recent news story. You could use the subjects in the newspaper clippings in Part A for ideas. Prepare to explain the news story briefly in the next session.

Extra Practice Unit 23

Part A Six polite questions were recorded at the front desk of a hotel. Use the information in the direct questions below to complete the polite questions, as they were recorded.

Direct questions
1 Are there any restrooms on this floor?
2 Which floor is the restaurant on?
3 Where's the nearest subway station?
4 What time does the first airport bus leave?
5 Where can I get a taxi?
6 Have my colleagues arrived yet?

Polite questions, as recorded
1 "Can you tell me _____?"
2 "Could you tell me _____?"
3 "I need to know _____."
4 "Do you know _____?"
5 "Can you tell me _____?"
6 "I'd like to know _____."

Part B Some more recordings were made in the hotel lobby. They contain polite words or phrases that people used in different situations. Look at the descriptions of the situations below and write the polite word or phrase that you think each person used.

1 A guest walked up to the front desk, wanting to speak to the receptionist. The receptionist was sitting down, facing in the opposite direction, working on a computer. What did the guest say to the receptionist to get his attention?
_____

2 A guest asked the receptionist a question, but the receptionist didn't hear exactly what the guest asked. What did the receptionist say?
_____

3 A porter was helping a guest to carry her luggage to the elevator. He needed to get past two people who were standing in the way, near the elevator. What did the porter say to the people?
_____

4 When the elevator doors opened, the porter invited the guest to go into the elevator first. What did he say to her?
_____

5 When the porter arrived at the guest's room with her bags, she thanked him for his help. What did he reply?
_____

Extra Practice Unit 24

Part A Fill in the missing words to complete the article.

A VISITOR'S GUIDE TO EATING IN BRITISH PUBS

The word "pub" is short for "public house". But what, exactly, is a pub? A **1 b**_____ where people go for a drink? A place to eat? Generally, the answer is a bit of both. All pubs sell drinks and many also **2 c**_____ food. Often, dishes are called bar **3 m**_____, which means you eat them in the bar.

If you want some food, don't sit down in a pub and wait for someone to come to your table and bring you a **4 m**_____. You need to go to the bar and get one yourself. You can buy a drink at the same time. Again, drinks are not **5 s**_____ at tables in pubs – you have to get them from the bar. Once you've chosen what you want, go to the bar and **6 o**_____ your food. Then, when the food is ready, it will be brought from the **7 k**_____ to your table.

When it comes to settling the check – called the **8 b**_____ in the UK – there are different ways of doing things. Sometimes, you **9 p**_____ in advance at the bar, before the meal. Sometimes, you settle after the meal, usually at the bar. And, since service is minimal, there's no need to leave a **10 t**_____.

After saying all this, some pubs that serve food also have a separate dining room. In pubs like these, customers who wish to eat are taken to a table in the dining room. Then orders are taken and food is served by a **11 w**_____ – as in a traditional **12 r**_____.

Part B Are these sentences about pubs true or false?

1. Bar meals are usually listed on a menu.   T   F
2. Orders for bar meals are normally taken at the table, by a waiter.   T   F
3. Generally, bar meals are collected from the kitchen by the customer.   T   F
4. When you pay for a bar meal, always leave an extra payment for service.   T   F
5. Some pubs have a restaurant in another room, away from the bar.   T   F

Part C Imagine you're giving some advice to a foreign friend or colleague by email about eating out in your country. Write two or three paragraphs explaining what to do in a restaurant or in another type of food outlet you know about. Talk about the points below.

- arriving at the restaurant and getting a table
- ordering the different courses of the meal
- paying the bill/check

Extra Practice Unit 25

Part A Use the correct forms of the words below to complete the article.

advertise   fall   rise

THE EVER-CHANGING WORLD OF ADVERTISING

How has the world of 1 a _____ changed over the years? It seems that there are more 2 a _____ today than ever before. We get this impression because goods and services are 3 a _____ in more ways than in the past – not just in print, and in TV and radio commercials, but also now on the web, by email, in text messages and in all kinds of other ways.

Do companies really 4 a _____ more today? Has their spending on marketing 5 r _____ over, say, the last 20 years? The answer is no. In fact, at some points during tough economic times in the past, spending actually 6 f _____.

The main trend in spending has been a steady move away from some areas toward others. Most notably, spending on marketing in the printed media (newspapers and magazines) has 7 f _____, while spending on Internet marketing has done the exact opposite. The 8 r _____ in Internet spending has mirrored the 9 f _____ in printed media spending. It's thought that, in the US, marketing spending on the Internet 10 r _____ above spending on printed media for the first time in 2011.

Part B Are these sentences about advertising true or false?

1 Today, there are more types of advertising than there used to be.   T   F
2 These days, companies spend more on advertising than they used to.   T   F
3 Advertising in the printed media includes TV and radio commercials.   T   F
4 Companies spend less on newspaper ads than they used to.   T   F
5 American companies now spend more on Internet ads than on newspaper ads.   T   F
6 The article says that spending on TV commercials has increased.   T   F

Part C Think about 1–5 below. Make notes and prepare to discuss the points in the next session.

1 Think of a product or service you bought – recently or in the past – after seeing it advertised.

2 Can you remember where you saw the ad or commercial?

3 Why did the ad/commercial get your attention?

4 Did you see the ad once or several times before you decided to make your purchase?

5 Based on this experience and any others you remember, what do you think makes ads effective?

Extra Practice Unit 26

Part A Use the words below to complete the article.

account   almost   cash   earn   estate   market   over   savings   sold   withdraw

INVESTMENT:
TIME AND TIMING

According to the saying, "Time is money". However, in investment you could say that a slightly different word is more important: timing. To **1** _____ the best return on your **2** _____, you need to put them in the right place at the right time. You also need to be ready to **3** _____ your money from one type of investment – for example, from stocks – and move it to another – into real **4** _____, for instance – at just the right moment.

Let's look at an example of an investor who started with $10,000 on August 12, 1982. On that day, the Dow Jones Industrial Average closed at 777 points, a low point after a long period of instability. After investing the money on the stock **5** _____, our investor did nothing for 17½ years – until January 14, 2000, when the Dow Jones ended an incredible rise to reach 11,723 points. On this day, our investor's initial $10,000 investment was worth just **6** _____ $150,000.

After correctly guessing that stocks had peaked and were about to begin a period of decline, our investor **7** _____ her shares and used the money to buy an apartment. She then waited again. By 2007, her $150,000 apartment was worth nearly $300,000, after property prices had **8** _____ doubled in just seven years. At this point, after correctly guessing that property had peaked, she sold the apartment and put the **9** _____ in her bank **10** _____. Before discounting inflation, over that period our investor had multiplied her money by about 30. This impressive performance was achieved partly thanks to time, but mostly thanks to timing.

Part B Complete these sentences with the correct numbers. Use the information in the article.

1 When the investor first invested her savings, the Dow Jones was at _____ points.
2 Between August 1982 and January 2000, the Dow Jones rose by almost _____ points.
3 The investor moved $ _____ out of stocks, into property.
4 The investor's savings were invested for a total period of nearly _____ years.
5 Over the whole period, the investor earned a total of $ _____.

Part C Now write the numbers from Part B in words.

1 _____ points
2 _____ points
3 _____ dollars
4 _____ years
5 _____ dollars

Extra Practice Unit 27

Part A Use each of the words below once to complete the customer reviews.

Feelings: annoying   awesome   disappointed   funny   glad   terrible
Linking words: also   although   either   however   so   too

Review 1

The description on the back cover looked excellent, so my hopes were high. Unfortunately, when I started reading I was quickly **1** _____ . I won't say the advice is **2** _____ , because there are some good tips in it. **3** _____ , a lot of the points are fairly obvious – you don't learn that much. **4** _____ , many of the tips are repeated several times, and this becomes **5** _____ after a while. **6** _____ I wasn't particularly satisfied with this. The price wasn't cheap, **7** _____ . I'm **8** _____ I didn't buy the hardcover version, which is even more expensive.

Review 2

This is truly **9** _____ – by far the best thing I've watched all year. Some of the scenes made me laugh out loud, and I never do that unless something is really **10** _____ . The extra material (deleted scenes, interviews with the actors) is excellent, **11** _____ – **12** _____ it's a pity there wasn't more of it. There seemed to be less of this kind of material than you normally get, which is why I haven't given it a top rating.

Part B What sort of product is each review about?

Review 1: a _____
Review 2: a _____

Part C Each of the reviews above was given a star rating, between zero and five. How many stars do you think each review received?

Review 1:   1 2 3 4 5
Review 2:   1 2 3 4 5

Part D Are these sentences about Review 1 true or false?

1 Before receiving the product, the person thought it would be good.   T   F
2 None of the advice is useful because all of it is obvious.   T   F
3 Some of the advice is covered more than once.   T   F
4 The person learned some new things.   T   F
5 The person bought the hardcover version, which cost more.   T   F

Part E Write a short review of a product you bought. Include good and bad points. Use some of the language from the reviews in Part A.

Extra Practice Unit 28

Part A Use each of the words below once to complete the article.

actor   character   documentary   movie   part   play   program   script   story   writer

THE ART OF MIXING FANTASY AND REALITY ON THE SCREEN

In the world of cinema and television, two new genres have become popular in recent years: docudrama and docufiction. The terms combine the word **1** _documentary_ with the words "drama" and "fiction" to describe a TV **2** _program_ or a **3** _movie_ that's a mixture of reality and fantasy.

The principle of both genres is that they're always based on a true **4** _story_. Every main **5** _character_ is also based on a real person – although a professional **6** _actor_ is employed to **7** _play_ each **8** _part_.
While the two genres are similar, a docudrama closely follows what really happened. With docufiction, the **9** _writer_ will be more creative when he or she writes the **10** _script_ in order to make it as entertaining as possible – although without going too far away from what really happened.

Part B Look at the descriptions below. Do they describe docudrama, docufiction or both? Mark the boxes. Use the information in the article to help you.

	Docudrama	Docufiction
1 The program is about something that really happened.	☐	☐
2 The people in the story are based on real individuals.	☐	☐
3 Above all, the program must be very realistic.	☐	☐
4 Real events can be changed a little to improve the story.	☐	☐
5 A script is produced by a writer, for the actors.	☐	☐

Part C Find words in the completed article to fill in the gaps below. Sometimes, more than one word is possible.

1 A script is produced by a _____.
2 The script shows what the _____ should say.
3 The script tells the _____ of what happened.
4 A _____ is about real facts or events.
5 _____ means something that's not true.

Part D Have you ever watched a docudrama or docufiction? If so, prepare to briefly discuss what it's about in the next session.

Extra Practice Unit 29

Part A Fill in the missing words to complete the article.

The Instant Sleep Solution

It's a common sight at any airport: tired, jetlagged travelers in the departure area trying to sleep – on benches, on their bags, on the floor – usually somewhere pretty **1 u_____**. Of course, there are usually hotels at large airports. But there's not much point in paying for a full night's **2 a_____** if you just need a couple of hours' sleep. And if you haven't booked a room in **3 a_____**, it will probably cost you a fortune to **4 c_____** into a hotel – if you can find one that has **5 v_____**.

The problem of finding quiet, secure places to sleep in public areas, such as airports, may soon be a thing of the past, however. The "Sleep Box", an invention by a Russian company, the Arch Group, is a compartment that offers a personal space to sleep.

It contains two comfortable **6 b_____**, a **7 d_____** where you can sit and work, and there's space to store your **8 l_____**.

Part B Use suitable words from the article above to complete the sentences below.

1 Sleeping on the floor or on a bench is not very _____.
2 People who just need to sleep for a short time don't want to pay for a hotel _____.
3 "Sleep Boxes" are soundproof, so they're _____ inside.
4 "Sleep Boxes" are _____, so there's no risk of having your bags stolen while you sleep.
5 A "Sleep Box" is large enough to accommodate two people and their _____.

Part C Look at another extract, below, from the same article. Then think about these questions. Make notes and prepare to discuss them in the next session.

"Sleep Boxes" have been tested at Moscow Airport, and the feedback from people who've used them has been positive. So will we soon see them in airport terminals around the world? The answer depends on a number of different issues.
- In your opinion, what issues will affect whether the "Sleep Box" is successful?
- Do you think the "Sleep Box" will be a global success?

Extra Practice Unit 30

Part A Use each of the words below once to complete the article.

around | as | away | below | down | of | off | on | over | through | to | up

THE STRANGE WORLD OF TITAN

Who's never dreamed of walking on the moon? The idea of jumping **1** _____ and floating gently **2** _____ the lunar surface is an amazing thought. However, our own moon is just one of at least 166 moons in the solar system. And some of them are much more interesting than our own. One such place is Titan, which is one of 62 moons orbiting the planet Saturn. Titan is much farther **3** _____ from the sun than the earth is, and **4** _____ a result has a surface temperature of −179 °C (−290 °F), which is of course far **5** _____ the freezing point of water. However, Titan is thought to be the only place in the solar system, other than earth, that has large lakes of liquid on its surface – although that liquid is not water, but methane (carbon and hydrogen).

Titan is also unique because it's the only moon that's known to have an atmosphere **6** _____ it – although it is not thought to contain oxygen, so it is not air that humans could breathe. The atmosphere on Titan is much denser ("thicker") than the earth's atmosphere. Because **7** _____ this and due **8** _____ the moon's very weak gravity compared with earth, it is said that if humans stood **9** _____ the surface of Titan with wings on their arms, by flapping them up and **10** _____, they could take **11** _____ and fly **12** _____ the atmosphere like birds.

Part B Are the sentences below true or false?

1. Titan is Saturn's only moon. T F
2. Compared with the earth, Titan is closer to the sun. T F
3. The lakes on Titan are made of ice. T F
4. It's thought that just one moon in the solar system has an atmosphere. T F
5. Titan's atmosphere is exactly the same as the earth's atmosphere. T F
6. There is gravity on Titan. T F

Part C Use the information in the article to complete these sentences about Titan.

1. Water would freeze on Titan as a result to _____.
2. It would be easy to fly on Titan due to _____.
3. It would take years to travel from earth to Titan because of _____.
4. Titan is a unique moon because of _____.

Notes

Listening Texts

Unit 16

Listening 16.1 (Track 1)

Woman:
As someone who reads a lot, I think the concept of electronic publishing is great – although, personally, I don't have an electronic book reader. In my opinion, e-books will definitely continue to grow in popularity, because of the obvious advantages they offer. Although I'm not sure whether electronic copies will ever replace paper copies. I'd say we'll continue to have paper books for a very long time, and maybe forever.

I'm sure music will become one hundred percent electronic. That's definitely going to happen before too long. But I don't think books will go in the same direction. Because they're physical things – you hold them in your hands. So they're not the same as music. But that's just my point of view. Maybe I'm old-fashioned!

Listening 16.2 (Track 2)

Woman: Well, I don't really agree that paper books are an "endangered species". As I said before, I'm not sure whether e-books will ever replace paper ones. I think people will always want paper copies, with pages they can turn.
Man: Sure. Books have existed for centuries. They're not going to just disappear. That's a ridiculous idea.
Woman: Definitely. And I think the suggestion that all books will contain video is ridiculous, as well. Surely, people will still want to read ordinary books.
Man: Absolutely. Basically, I totally disagree with everything in this blog. But reading it is quite amusing, because it's a great example of the kind of nonsense you often read in stuff that people publish on the web.
Woman: True.
Man: Just look what he's written about paper books disappearing. "I'm not sure I agree that the change will happen in ten years. It'll probably take 15." So he thinks he can predict something like that to the nearest five years! It just shows how credible his views are …

Listening 16.3 (Track 3)

1
Woman: People will start buying all their music as pop videos.
2
Man: Movie theaters can't survive in a world with VCRs.
3
Man: In twenty years all homes will have a computer.
4
Woman: I can't imagine cell phones becoming very popular.
5
Man: One day all computers will be linked together by phone.

Unit 17

Listening 17.1 (Track 4)

A: I'll phone you sometime next week.
B: I'll call you later and give you the details.
C: I just need to make a phone call.
D: I'll give you a call as soon as I get home.
E: I'll give you a ring from the airport.

Listening 17.2 (Track 5)

Part A

1 Your call will be taken in a moment. BEEP.
2
A: Hello?
B: Hello, is Andreas there, please?
A: Yes. He's standing right next to me. BEEP.
C: Hello.
3
A: Hello. Adam?
B: Yes. BEEP.
A: Hi there, it's …
4
A: Can I speak to Mr. Tanaka, please?
B: He's on the phone at the moment. BEEP.
A: Oh, right. OK, I'll …
5
A: I can't really talk now. I'm halfway through my lunch.
B: Oh, sorry.
A: No problem. BEEP.
B: Sure.

Listening Texts

Part B (Track 6)

1 Your call will be taken in a moment. Please hold.
2
A: Hello?
B: Hello. Is Andreas there, please?
A: Yes. He's standing right next to me. I'll put him on.
C: Hello.
3
A: Hello. Adam?
B: Yes. Speaking.
A: Hi there, it's …
4
A: Can I speak to Mr. Tanaka, please?
B: He's on the phone at the moment. The line's busy.
A: Oh, right. OK, I'll …
5
A: I can't really talk now. I'm halfway through my lunch.
B: Oh, sorry.
A: No problem. Can I call you back?
B: Sure.

Listening 17.3 (Track 7)

1
Woman: Is it possible to fly direct to Sydney?
2
Man: Can you get a bus to the airport?
3
Woman: How long does it take to fly to Cape Town?
4
Man: Where's the main airport in New Zealand?

Unit 18

Listening 18.1 (Track 8)

Benjamin:
I think the first question is, can you really compare modern gadgets with old-fashioned ones? And I'd say you can't. Cell phones are a good example. You can't compare a modern smartphone with an old-fashioned telephone. A smartphone has got so many more functions than an old-fashioned phone. So you can't say that one's more complicated than the other, because they're completely different products – they're not comparable.

But the question of complexity and simplicity is an important one. It's true that, as gadgets such as smartphones get more and more functions, there's a danger they become too complicated. And that's the challenge for engineers like me. We have to offer functions that are sophisticated, but simple to use at the same time. And achieving that … is far from simple!

Listening 18.2 (Track 9)

1 Plug in the power adapter.
2 Take off the battery cover.
3 Take out the battery.
4 Put on the battery cover.
5 Put in the battery.

Listening 18.3 (Track 10)

1 The only way to make the tablet work is to plug it in.
2 You have to leave the plug in. The power cuts off if you pull it out.
3 If the tablet isn't plugged in, then you can't turn it on.
4 I'm not sure if I should leave the battery in, or take it out.

Unit 19

Listening 19.1 (Track 11)
Part A

Interviewer: So what's the main advantage of doing a big interior renovation?
Astrid: Well, the obvious advantage is that you can personalize your home – you can make it suit your own needs and your own tastes.
Interviewer: And the main disadvantage?
Astrid: Well, if you're living in the property while the work's going on, the big problem is the mess. Especially if you're doing the kitchen or the bathroom – those two rooms are the most problematic, because replacing bathtubs and sinks and tiles and things like that is a big job.

Listening Texts

It takes a lot longer than just redecorating the living room or a bedroom. And also, if the kitchen and bathroom are a mess, it makes it hard to do essential everyday things – it's difficult to wash, and to cook meals.

Interviewer: What about cost? Are renovations worth the money?

Part C (Track 12)

Interviewer: What about the cost? Is renovating worth it, financially?

Astrid: That's a good question. It depends. If the interior is in a bad state, and as a result of that you buy your property for a cheaper price, then it can be worth it, financially. But you have to be careful. People generally underestimate the cost of renovations. So the work will probably cost much more than you think. And it also depends on whether you're getting builders in to do the work for you, or doing it yourself. Obviously, it can be a lot cheaper if you do the work yourself. So that's an important consideration, too.

Listening 19.2 (Track 13)
Part B

Astrid:
Historically, when people chose building materials, they used what was in the local environment. People used the materials they could find nearby: stones from the hills, wood from the forests, and so on. That's where styles of building come from. And often, those styles are still here today. So, as an architect, you try to follow traditional, local styles. And even in modern cities, where new types of building have developed, you still try to follow the style of that part of the city. If you're building an office block in a business district, where there's lots of concrete and glass, you tend to use those kinds of materials. So, really, the biggest thing is the local style – buildings have to fit in. You know, you could construct a beautiful stone house, but if you built it in a neighborhood where all the other houses were in brick, it would look awful.

Listening 19.3 (Track 14)

Guide:
As you can see, the stone carving at the tops of the columns is very complex. This is a style called Corinthian. It's one of the three traditional styles used in stone columns. The other two styles are called Ionic and Doric. And as you can also see, a lot of the stone in the facade is very dark – it's almost black in parts. Now that's not because it's dirty. It's actually because the stone contains iron …

Unit 20

Listening 20.1 (Track 15)

Man:
I'm not one of these people who always pay their bills at the last minute. I hate admin, so I prefer to sort out payments and things like that immediately, to get them out of the way. As soon as I've paid bills, I file them in boxes and put them away in a closet, out of sight. And, if there are any papers I don't need, I just throw them out. I hate to see paperwork lying around.

Listening 20.2 (Track 16)

Tom:
When you're doing a very physical job, such as digging with a spade, working harder doesn't mean digging faster. Don't dig like crazy and tire yourself out in an hour. If you work less quickly, you'll do more in a day.

And, when you dig with a pickaxe, never lift it higher than your shoulders. Pickaxes work better and are much less tiring to work with when you swing them less aggressively and use them more carefully. By keeping the tool low, you'll also work a lot more safely.

Listening 20.3 (Track 17)

Ellie:
In the sixties, I'd say the job that used to take a lot longer, compared with today, was doing the laundry. I had a washing machine, so I could wash my laundry with that. But the old machine I used to have was nothing like the ones you see today. You couldn't just put the laundry in, turn it on and leave it. You used to have to fill it with water through a hose. Then you couldn't start it up immediately – the water took time to heat

133

up. Then, once the water was hot, you put the laundry in – into the top of the machine. And then you could leave it to wash everything – that part was automatic. But when it had finished washing, you had to take the laundry out while it was still soaking wet. The old machine couldn't spin the water out like modern ones can. So you used to have water dripping all over the place. Then you had to empty the water out of the machine into the sink, through the hose. So … it used to be much harder work.

Unit 21

Listening 21.1 (Track 18)

1 It's difficult to find your way around the airport.
2 We won't be able to get there on time.
3 It's impossible to get a refund with this type of ticket.
4 The trouble is, if you buy a ticket for immediate travel, it's really expensive.
5 I don't think you will be able to get a seat on the flight.

Listening 21.2 (Track 19)
Part A

1 We could go by train and then rent a car when we get there.
2 How about getting a taxi to the hotel? It'll be quicker than waiting for the bus.
3 Shall we book seats next to each other, so we can work on the train?
4 What about booking the hotel with the flight? We'll probably get a cheaper deal.
5 Why don't we drive through the night, so we miss all the traffic?

Part B (Track 20)

1
A: We could go by train and then rent a car when we get there.
B: Good idea. I'd prefer to avoid driving all that way …
2
A: How about getting a taxi to the hotel? It'll be quicker than waiting for the bus.
B: Wouldn't it be better to walk? It's only five or ten minutes from here …

3
A: Shall we book seats next to each other, so we can work on the train?
B: That sounds good, yeah. We may as well use the time …
4
A: What about booking the hotel with the flight? We'll probably get a cheaper deal.
B: OK, let's do that. We can take a look on …
5
A: Why don't we drive through the night, so we miss all the traffic?
B: Why not? I'd rather miss a night's sleep than get stuck …

Part C (Track 21)

1 Good idea.
2 Wouldn't it be better to walk?
3 That sounds good.
4 OK, let's do that.
5 Why not?

Listening 21.3 (Track 22)

1 … they didn't manage to get them going.
2 … the pilots managed to start one engine.

Unit 22

Listening 22.1 (Track 23)

1 The trouble here is that there aren't enough houses and apartments to meet demand. So the cost of buying a place or renting a place is sky-high. And that's why there are so many homeless people living on the streets.
2 And the last recession didn't help the situation. Unemployment is still over ten percent here, so there are a lot of people out of work. And if you're poor in this area, it's especially tough. The cost of living is just too high.
3 And that obviously results in people stealing, it results in violence. I'm not saying being poor is an excuse for doing that kind of thing, but poverty is obviously one of the big causes. And at the end of the day, having more police officers or building more jails doesn't do anything about the cause of the problem.

Listening Texts

4   I think public money would be better spent on building hospitals, and employing more doctors and nurses. There are people who have to wait months to get medical care, and patients who can't afford to get the drugs they need. Surely doing something about that should be a priority.

Listening 22.2 (Track 24)

A: Is there anywhere near here where I can get something to eat? I've been walking around for ages. I've looked everywhere.
B: I'm afraid there's nowhere to get food here. You'd have to go into town. What sort of place are you looking for? A restaurant? A snack bar?
A: It doesn't matter. Anywhere, really. The nearest place there is.
B: There's somewhere just next to the train station where you can get sandwiches. I think that's the nearest place from here. I don't know anywhere closer than that.

Listening 22.3 (Track 25)

1
Let me show you on the map. So the museum's here. And just across the street there's the main art gallery. And then the park's at the end of the street, here. It's only a short walk. And the statues shown on the photos on the last page are all in this park. So there's quite a lot to see …

2
What do you want to do? There are quite a few cafes and bars along this next street. We could go to one of those. Or, if you prefer, we could get a takeout and have it back at the office. It's up to you, whatever you want …

3
A: This is the theater we went to last time you came, if you remember – where we went to see the opera.
B: Yes, I recognize it. So what's on at the moment?
A: Ballet, according to the poster.
B: Right. And is this where you came for that concert?
A: No, that was in the sports stadium. They do have some concerts here, but it's too small for big pop concerts. They usually have those at the stadium …

Unit 23

Listening 23.1 (Track 26)

1   Have a safe trip back.
2   Excuse me. Your suitcase is blocking the door.
3   Thanks for your help.
4   Sorry I'm late.
5   It's a bad line. I'm just calling to … tomorrow.
6   Here's your coffee. And I've booked you a taxi for 4 o'clock. And I've also made you a snack to take with you on the trip.

Listening 23.2 (Track 27)

1   Excuse me. Do you know if there's a subway station near here?
2   Excuse me. Can you tell me when the next bus is?
3   Excuse me. Do you know what time it is?
4   Excuse me. Can you tell me whether this ticket is still valid?

Listening 23.3 (Track 28)

Jo:
I think the best example of cultural difference is how friendly people seem to be. Because there's no such thing as a culture where it's normal to be unfriendly. Friendliness is a basic human value. The question is, how do people show that they're friendly? And there are different ways to do that in different cultures.

So, in some cultures, people show friendliness by being open. So when they meet people for the first time, they're outgoing, they talk freely about themselves and they ask other people about themselves. So the message they try to send is, I'm open, I'm relaxed, I'm prepared to share things about myself with you, like a friend.

Whereas in other cultures, when people meet for the first time, friendliness is shown, not by openness, but by respect. So people make an effort not to ask personal questions and not to talk too much. Because they don't want to make the other person feel uncomfortable. So in that culture, if you're very open and very outgoing, it's seen as invasive.

Unit 24

Listening 24.1 (Track 29)

Guest: Excuse me. Is there anywhere near here where we can get a quick lunch?
Receptionist: A quick lunch. You're in a hurry.
Guest: We are.
Receptionist: Do you want to sit down to eat, or get a snack to take out?
Guest: I guess we'd prefer to sit down. Is there anywhere where the service is fairly fast?
Receptionist: Well there's a place just around the corner. They have a self-service buffet – there are no waiters. You just take a tray, get what you want, then go and pay.
Guest: That sounds good.
Receptionist: It gets busy there at lunchtime – it's very popular. But it should be fairly quiet now – it's quite early.
Guest: That sounds great. So it's just around the corner?
Receptionist: Yes, if you go out of the door and turn left …

Listening 24.2 (Track 30)

1 seafood
2 poultry
3 vegetarian
4 spicy
5 alcohol
6 appetizer
7 dessert
8 portion
9 menu

Listening 24.3 (Track 31)

1
A: Would you mind passing me the salt, please?
B: Here you are.
A: Thanks. Ah. That's the pepper.
B: Oh sorry! There you are.
A: Thank you …

2
A: Excuse me. Would it be possible to have a knife and fork? I'm not very good at using chopsticks.
B: No problem. One moment.
A: Thanks very much …

3
A: Well, this is delicious. You made a great recommendation.
B: Thank you.
A: I had no idea what to choose, so I'm glad you helped me out …

4
A: Would anybody like some more?
B: Yes, please.
A: The dish is hot. Careful.
B: Thank you.
A: There's the spoon. Help yourself. There you are.
B: Thanks …

5
A: Dessert?
B: No, thanks. Can we just have the check, please?
A: Yes, fine.

Talking Point 24 (Track 32)

Harry:
Well, you need many, many ingredients to make a good restaurant – there are so many things that you shouldn't neglect. But if I had to choose one, I would say the most important thing is to offer good value for money. It's obvious you need to serve good food – but I think the definition of "good food" is "good food relative to the price".

Because, think about it. What happens in a restaurant? You go in, you look at the menu and you choose a dish. And when you choose a dish – before the waiter brings it – you know how much it's going to cost, because the price is on the menu. And that price gives you certain expectations. If the price is high, then your expectations are high. If the price is low, then your expectations are fairly low. And that means that when the waiter brings the meal it can be worse than you expected – in which case you'll be disappointed – or it can be better than you expected – in which case you'll be pleasantly surprised.

And that feeling – pleasant surprise, or disappointment – will stay with you, like a taste in your mouth. You'll remember that feeling long after you've left the restaurant. So if your customers are pleasantly surprised and feel they've had good value for money, they'll tell other people about your great restaurant. It's pretty simple – but at the end of the day, that's how it works.

Listening Texts

Unit 25

Listening 25.1 (Track 33)

Hanna:
If you look at all six of these ads, they all contain the same message. Terms like "sale", "special offer", "25% off", "free", "half-price", "win" – they all mean that you'll save money ... either because the price is lower, or because you can get something, or something extra, without having to pay for it. So they all send out the message – "Save money".

And there's another message in three of the ads. And that message is, "Buy quickly". So in the "Sale" poster, it says that the sale ends on January 28th. So in other words, hurry up and buy – the sale ends soon. In the ad for half-price fares, it says "Limited seats available, book now". Another ad says "Subscribe now". So the message is, "Don't delay – this offer will end soon".

Listening 25.2 (Track 34)

1 When you're buying something expensive, I think it's dangerous to be in a hurry. It's important to take your time ... to give yourself the time to compare different products and make sure you compare prices. And try not to make a quick decision. Go home, think about it, sleep on it and decide the next day.
2 I'd say, make sure you get as much independent advice as you can. Read reviews on the web from people who've bought the product. Mention to friends and family that you're planning to buy a new ... whatever it is. They might just say something interesting – tell you about a good store they know, or about a bad experience they had. It's important to get as much information as you can. Then you can use that to make your decision.

Listening 25.3 (Track 35)

1 When new TVs come out, older models get cheaper.
2 Most experts predict that in the long-term, oil will get more expensive.
3 Over the years, the technology used in cars has gotten better.
4 As furniture has become cheaper, its quality has gotten worse.
5 The global market for cell phones is getting bigger.

Unit 26

Listening 26.1 (Track 36)
Part B

Man:
The government stepped in to save the banks last time, but from what I've heard, if there's another crisis they might not be able to afford to do it again. But what would be the consequences if my bank failed? Well, personally, I wouldn't really care. And the reason is, I have a mortgage, so I owe the bank money. OK, I've got some savings, so the bank also owes me a bit. But the amount I still owe on the mortgage is more than my savings. So if the bank failed, overall I wouldn't lose. In fact, maybe I'd win! That's the way I look at it ...

Listening 26.2 (Track 37)

Narrator:
Back in 2007, I sold my apartment for double the price I paid for it in 1998. When I bought the place, I thought it cost a fortune. But it was easy to get a mortgage at the time – the bank lent me the money without problem. Then, just after that, real-estate prices shot up. I think they rose by a 100% in six or seven years. It was a crazy time – there was so much demand. I remember, I put my apartment on the market and within one week I got three offers for it.

So I made a lot of money on the sale – and at the same time I withdrew my money from the market. Then I rented another apartment while I was looking for a new home, as it was difficult to find places – as I said, there was so much demand. And then, suddenly the real-estate bubble burst. That was it. Prices fell. So I just waited. I knew there was no point buying in a falling market. In the end, I waited three and a half years. Eventually, I found a house I really liked, so I took the opportunity and went for it. I spent about 30% less than it was worth in 2007. That was in 2010, so it was before prices hit rock bottom. I guess the house lost some value just after that – but not too much.

So here's some advice from someone who won in the real-estate lottery: buy at the bottom of the market, sell at the top, wait for prices to fall, then buy again. And the key to perfect timing? Luck!

Listening 26.3
Part A (Track 38)

1. the twenty-first century
2. nineteen ninety-nine
3. fourteen thousand one hundred and sixtyfour
4. two thousand and seven
5. nine point three percent
6. one hundred and fifty thousand tons
7. six trillion dollars
8. six hundred and fifty million tons
9. four hundred billion dollars
10. zero point zero two three percent

Part B (Track 39)

1. the Dow Jones Industrial Average went from eleven thousand four hundred and ninety-seven at the end of nineteen ninety-nine
2. a low of six thousand five hundred and forty-seven in two thousand and nine
3. to close the decade at ten thousand four hundred and twenty-eight
4. The cereal grew in value by roughly two hundred and fifty percent.
5. gold is approximately one thousand five hundred percent more valuable than the world's wheat

Unit 27

Listening 27.1 (Track 40)

Woman 1: It was brilliant! I was nervous before we set off. But as soon as we got going it was fantastic. I want to go back and do it again!
Man 1: There was a long line of people, so I almost didn't bother to wait. But I'm glad I did. It was awesome.
Man 2: That was scary. I had my eyes closed the whole time. But I'm pleased I did it. I didn't think I'd dare to do it, so I'm satisfied I found the courage.
Woman 2: It was funny watching my sister sitting next to me. She looked more scared than I was. I thought it was fun.

Listening 27.2 (Track 41)

Researcher: What did you think of the quality of the food?
Customer: Well, for me, the question wasn't about quality, it was about choice – or the lack of choice. There's only one place to get food. We had to wait for ages to get served. And there were only about … I don't know … four or five things on the menu. And there were only two options for children. I can't believe that an amusement park – which is mainly for kids – only has two types of children's meal available. And, to make things worse, you're not allowed to bring your own food and drink into the park. So … I'm pretty angry about that.

Listening 27.3 (Track 42)

1
A: I had a good day. The weather was good, too.
B: I had a good day. But the weather wasn't very good.

2
A: The hotel was great. It was cheap, as well.
B: The hotel was great. Although it was expensive.

3
A: There are tickets available. We also have some reduced fares.
B: There are tickets available. However, we only have full-price fares.

Unit 28

Listening 28.1 (Track 43)

Sabrina:
One of the easiest kinds of programs to make adaptations for is documentaries, especially the kind that doesn't have a presenter on screen, which is common in wildlife documentaries. In a program like that, the only voice you have is the narrator. So that voice can easily be replaced by a narrator who speaks the local language.

But even in other sorts of documentaries where people are interviewed, there are no real problems. One solution is simply to translate what the person says and put subtitles on the screen for people to read. Or another possibility is, the voice of an interpreter can be dubbed over the voice of the person in the interview. And both of those options are acceptable to viewers because they're used to subtitles and dubbing when foreign people are interviewed – it's a normal style of television journalism.

Then there are other types of programs that are much more difficult to translate. Comedy shows are certainly the most difficult to adapt. It can be done. Some American sitcoms have been dubbed in other languages very successfully. But adapting situation comedy – or any type of comedy – has to be done very expertly.

Listening 28.2 (Track 44)

1 guitar   6 banjo
2 piano   7 recorder
3 violin   8 trombone
4 trumpet   9 bagpipes
5 saxophone   10 accordion

Listening 28.3
Part B (Track 45)

Man:
In my opinion, the problem with watching a movie after you've read the novel is that … it's different. Generally, the characters and the places are not how you imagined them, in your own mind, when you read the book.

The other problem is, the story in the movie is always a bit different from the book. In the movie, there are generally parts that are left out.

So I'm often disappointed with movie adaptations. But that doesn't stop me from going to see movie versions of books I've read. I'm always fascinated to find out what they're like.

Part C (Track 46)

Man:
But there is one classic movie trilogy I watched, which is based on a classic novel I read – I've actually read it twice. And I was really impressed with the film.

The actors who played the main parts were all similar to the way I imagined the characters in the book. So that was a positive.

The special effects were very good, as well – the story's set in a world full of strange creatures and monsters, and I thought they all looked real. The special effects were great.

The locations where they shot the movie were also very well chosen – there are lots of scenes with mountains and spectacular landscapes, and they all looked good on screen, the way you imagine them when you read the book.

And also, the whole movie – which is in three parts – is really long. They didn't cut out lots of stuff from the novel, which is a very long book – or, rather, three very long books.

So they did a great job. And the name of the movie, and the novel, as you've probably guessed, is …

Unit 29

Listening 29.1 (Track 47)

Person 1:
It was packed. When the manager came out and showed us where to pitch, I couldn't believe it – there was just this tiny space between all these other tents. And there were people lighting stoves and cooking between them. It was quite dangerous.

Person 2:
The room was quite big, but there was no bathroom in it. You had to use the communal bathroom at the end of the corridor. And it was just bed and breakfast – they didn't serve food the rest of the day.

Person 3:
We booked half-board, so breakfast and dinner were included. Some people were staying full-board, so they were eating there at lunchtime as well. But it suited us better to eat out during the day.

Listening 29.2 (Track 48)

1 We ask you for a 30% deposit today, to confirm the booking. Then you pay the balance when you check out.
2 We've got no rooms free on the eighteenth – we're fully booked, I'm afraid. We have a vacancy on the nineteenth – I have a room free then.
3 You're canceling less than a week before the booking. So, because it's a last-minute cancellation, we can't give you a refund.
4 That's our bed-and-breakfast rate, so obviously breakfast is included.

Listening Texts

Listening 29.3 (Track 49)

Customer: Excuse me.
Receptionist: Yes.
Customer: There's a problem with the air-conditioning in my room. It's not working properly – it's blowing out freezing cold air, which is making the room really cold. And it won't stop. I've tried turning the dial to switch it off, but it won't turn. I'm not sure if it's the cause of the problem, but the plastic panel on the front's broken. It looks as if it's been hit with something.
Receptionist: Right. I'll arrange for somebody to…

Unit 30

Listening 30.1 (Track 50)

Umberto:
First, the spaceship's rockets lift it off the ground and push it upward, vertically. This takes it away from the earth and, eventually, into space. When the ship reaches space, it turns to become horizontal. Then its rockets push it until it reaches a very high speed. The ship's rockets then stop. Now, if the ship were still in the earth's atmosphere, it would slow down as it flew through the air – due to air resistance. But because there's no air in space, the ship doesn't slow down when its rockets stop. It keeps moving forward at the same speed.

Most people think that, above the earth, in space, there's no gravity. They think that's why astronauts are weightless. But that's not true. The earth's gravity continues to pull the spaceship and the astronauts downward. However, because the ship is moving so fast, as it falls it doesn't move toward the earth. Instead, it travels around the earth. So when a spaceship and its crew are in orbit, and weightless, they're actually constantly falling. And gravity is still pulling them.

Listening 30.2 (Track 51)

Umberto:
There's a risk that a very big space rock – an asteroid – could hit the earth. There are thousands of asteroids orbiting quite near the earth, and we think about a thousand of them are bigger than one kilometer, which is about two-thirds of a mile. If an asteroid of that size hit us, we believe it would cause an extinction event – in other words, most of life on the planet would be destroyed.

So, because of this danger, there's a telescope in Hawaii called the PS1 Observatory. "PS" stands for "Panoramic Survey". And one of the telescope's main jobs is to look for big asteroids heading for earth. But, due to all the stars in the sky, it's difficult to spot space rocks. They're just tiny lights, not as bright as stars. So the stars make them difficult to see.

So what they do at PS1 is to take a photograph of part of the night sky, and then, a short time after, they take another photo. Then they use computers to compare the two pictures and see if anything has moved. And, as a result of that comparison, they can spot moving rocks.

Listening 30.3 (Track 52)

1 They say travel broadens the mind.
2 They don't know exactly how many stars are in the Milky Way.
3 They say there are billions of galaxies.
4 They think most galaxies have hundreds of billions of stars.

Solutions to Listening Exercises

Unit 16

Listening 16.1
Part A

1 think 3 sure 5 sure 7 view
2 opinion 4 say 6 think

Part B
No model answers possible

Listening 16.2
Part A

1 She disagrees.
2 He also disagrees.
3 They're nonsense.

Part B

A don't really
B totally
C not sure

Strength of disagreement (strongest first):
B → A → C

Part C

1 sure 3 absolutely
2 definitely 4 true

Listening 16.3

1 She said people would start buying all their music as pop videos.
2 He said movie theaters couldn't survive in a world with VCRs.
3 He said in twenty years all homes would have a computer.
4 She said she couldn't imagine cell phones becoming very popular.
5 He said one day all computers would be linked together by phone.

Unit 17

Listening 17.1
Part A

1 to phone someone
2 to call someone
3 to give someone a call
4 to give someone a ring
5 to make a phone call

Part B

A I'll phone you sometime next week.
B I'll call you later and give you the details.
C I just need to make a phone call.
D I'll give you a call as soon as I get home.
E I'll give you a ring from the airport.

Listening 17.2
Part A

1 B 3 A 5 D
2 C 4 E

Part B
No model answers possible

Listening 17.3
Part A
No model answers possible

Part B
Possible answers
1 She asked if it's possible to fly direct to Sydney.
2 He asked whether you can go by bus to the airport.
3 She wants to know how long it takes to fly to Cape Town.
4 He asked me where the main airport in New Zealand is.

Unit 18

Listening 18.1
Possible answer
You can't really compare modern gadgets with old-fashioned ones. For example, a modern smartphone has a lot more functions than an old-fashioned phone. They're not comparable . Modern gadgets have to offer functions that are sophisticated , but simple to use.

Listening 18.2

1 in 3 out 5 in
2 off 4 on

Listening 18.3

1 in 2 out 3 on 4 out

Solutions to Listening Exercises

Unit 19

Listening 19.1
Part A
1. The main advantage is that you can personalize your home.
2. Mess.
3. The kitchen and bathroom, because replacing bathtubs, sinks, tiles, etc. is a big job. And, during the work, it's hard to do essential things like washing and cooking.

Part B
No model answers possible

Part C
Possible answer
If the interior is in a bad state, and, as a result, you buy the home for a cheaper price, it can be worth it, financially. But people often underestimate the cost of renovations, so the work often costs more than they think. The cost also depends on whether you get builders to do the work. It can be a lot cheaper if you do the work yourself.

Listening 19.2
Part A
No model answers possible

Part B
Possible answer
Historically, people used the materials they could find nearby. That's where local styles of building came from. Today, architects follow traditional, local styles. Also in modern cities, where new types of building have developed, they follow the style of that part of the city. Buildings have to fit in.

Listening 19.3
1. complex   2. traditional   3. dark

Unit 20

Listening 20.1
Part A
1. sort   3. file   5. away   7. out
2. out   4. put   6. throw

Part B
No model answers possible

Listening 20.2
Part A
1. harder   5. less aggressively
2. faster   6. more carefully
3. less quickly   7. more safely
4. better

Part B
No model answers possible

Listening 20.3
Part A
Possible answer
She had a washing machine, but it was nothing like the ones today. You used to fill it with water through a hose. When the water was hot, you put the laundry in. And, when it finished washing, you took the laundry out while it was still wet, then emptied the water into the sink, through the hose.

Part B
1. could   3. couldn't   5. couldn't
2. couldn't   4. could

Unit 21

Listening 21.1
1. difficult   3. impossible   5. be able to
2. be able to   4. trouble

Listening 21.2
Part A
Possible answers
1. We could go by train and then rent a car when we get there.
2. How about getting a taxi to the hotel? It'll be quicker than waiting for the bus.
3. Shall we book seats next to each other, so we can work on the train?
4. What about booking the hotel with the flight? We'll probably get a cheaper deal.
5. Why don't we drive through the night, so we miss all the traffic?

Part B
1. A   3. A   5. A
2. D   4. A

Solutions to Listening Exercises

Part C
1 Good idea.
2 Wouldn't it be better to walk?
3 That sounds good.
4 OK, let's do that.
5 Why not?

Listening 21.3
1 ... they didn't manage to get them going.
2 ... the pilots managed to start one engine.

Unit 22

Listening 22.1
Part A
1 C real estate
2 D the economy
3 A crime
4 B health

Part B
Possible answers
1 houses, apartments, renting, homeless
2 recession, unemployment, out of work, poor, cost of living
3 stealing, violence, police officers, jails
4 hospitals, doctors, nurses, medical care, patients, drugs

Listening 22.2
1 anywhere
2 everywhere
3 nowhere
4 Anywhere
5 somewhere
6 anywhere

Listening 22.3
Part A
1 C 2 A 3 B

Part B
1 museum, art gallery, statue
2 cafe, bar, takeout
3 theater, opera, ballet, concert, sports stadium, pop concert

Unit 23

Listening 23.1
Possible answers
1 Thanks. / Thank you.
2 Sorry.
3 You're welcome.
4 No problem.
5 Sorry? / Excuse me? / Pardon me?
6 Thanks a lot. / Thanks very much. / Thank you very much.

Listening 23.2
Part A
1 Excuse me. Do you know if there's a subway station near here?
2 Excuse me. Can you tell me when the next bus is?
3 Excuse me. Do you know what time it is?
4 Excuse me. Can you tell me whether this ticket is still valid?

Part B
No model answers possible

Listening 23.3
Part A
Possible answer
Culture 1: In some cultures, people are open. They talk freely about themselves and ask other people about themselves. This shows that they're happy to share things, like with a friend.
Culture 2: In other cultures, it's important to show respect. People make an effort not to ask personal questions because they don't want to make the other person feel uncomfortable. They don't want to seem invasive.

Part B
No model answers possible

Unit 24

Listening 24.1
Part A
1 Lunch.
2 No, the guest would prefer to sit down to eat.
3 A place with a self-service buffet.
4 The place gets busy at lunchtime. But it should be fairly quiet now, because it's quite early.

Solutions to Listening Exercises

Part B
1 take out 3 waiters 5 busy
2 service 4 tray 6 quiet

Listening 24.2
1 seafood
2 poultry
3 vegetarian
4 spicy
5 alcohol
6 appetizer
7 dessert
8 portion
9 menu

Listening 24.3
Part A
1 A 3 B 5 C
2 C 4 A

Part B
1 mind – B
2 possible – C
3 like – A

Part C
salt knife chopsticks spoon
pepper fork dish

Unit 25

Listening 25.1
Part A
No model answers possible

Part B
Possible answer
All six ads give the message: "You'll save money". This message is given by: sale, special offer, 25 % off, free, half-price, win.
And three of the ads give the message: "Buy quickly". In the "Sale" poster the message is, "Hurry up and buy – the sale ends soon". In the ad for half-price fares, it says, "Limited seats available, book now". Another ad says, "Subscribe now".

Listening 25.2
Part A
No model answers possible

Part B
Possible answers
1 It's dangerous to be in a hurry. It's important to take your time and make sure you compare products and prices. And try not to make a quick decision. Go home, sleep on it and decide the next day.
2 Make sure you get as much independent advice as you can. Read reviews on the web. Tell friends and family what you're planning to buy. They might tell you about a good store or about a bad experience.

Listening 25.3
1 … get cheaper.
2 … get more expensive.
3 … has gotten better.
4 … has gotten worse.
5 … is getting bigger.

Unit 26

Listening 26.1
Part A
No model answers possible

Part B
Possible answer
The man wouldn't care if his bank failed, because he owes the bank more money on his mortgage than the amount of savings he has in the bank. So, overall, he owes the bank money.

Listening 26.2
1 sold 9 put 17 found
2 paid 10 got 18 took
3 bought 11 made 19 went
4 thought 12 withdrew 20 spent
5 cost 13 said 21 hit
6 lent 14 burst 22 lost
7 shot 15 fell 23 won
8 rose 16 knew

Solutions to Listening Exercises

Listening 26.3
Part A
1. the twenty-first century
2. nineteen ninety-nine
3. fourteen thousand one hundred (and) sixty-four
4. two thousand (and) seven
5. nine point three percent
6. one hundred (and) fifty thousand tons
7. six trillion dollars
8. six hundred (and) fifty million tons
9. four hundred billion dollars
10. zero point zero two three percent

Part B
1. 11,497
2. 6,547
3. 10,428
4. 250
5. 1,500

Unit 27

Listening 27.1
Part A
brilliant   glad   pleased   funny
fantastic   awesome   satisfied   fun

Part B
It was brilliant.   It was fun.
It was fantastic.   I'm glad.
It was awesome.   I'm pleased.
It was funny.   I'm satisfied.

Listening 27.2
Part A
Possible answer
There was only one place to get food and you had to wait a long time to be served. There were only two things on the menu for children. And you weren't allowed to bring your own food and drink into the park.

Part B
B annoyed   J surprised
D disappointed

Listening 27.3
No model answers possible

Unit 28

Listening 28.1
Part A
Possible answers
1. Documentaries – especially those that don't have a presenter on screen.
2. The voice of the narrator can be replaced by a narrator who speaks the local language. In interviews, you can translate what the person says and put subtitles on the screen. Or the voice of an interpreter can be dubbed over to replace the voice of the person in the interview.
3. Comedy shows are difficult to adapt.

Part B
Possible answers
1. a person who presents/hosts a TV program
2. a person whose voice explains what's happening in a documentary
3. change one language to another
4. text at the bottom of a screen to translate a foreign language
5. a person who explains what a speaker of another language is saying
6. when the voice of a speaker of the local language is recorded over the voice of a speaker of a foreign language

Listening 28.2
1. gui tar
2. pi ano
3. vio lin
4. trum pet
5. sax ophone
6. ban jo
7. re cord er
8. trom bone
9. bag pipes
10. ac cor dion

Listening 28.3
Part A
No model answers possible

Part B
In the movie, the characters and places are generally not how you imagined them when you read the book. And, in the movie, some parts of the story are left out. So the man is often disappointed with movie adaptations.

Solutions to Listening Exercises

Part C
1 He was really impressed.
2 The actors who played the main parts were similar to how he imagined the characters. The special effects were very good. The locations where they shot the movie were good. They didn't cut lots of stuff from the novel.
3 The movie trilogy was *Lord of the Rings*.

Unit 29

Listening 29.1
Part A
1 B   2 C   3 A

Part B
Possible answers
A to pitch, tents, stoves
B communal bathroom, bed and breakfast
C half-board (= breakfast and dinner included), full-board (= breakfast, lunch and dinner included)

Listening 29.2
Part A
1 dates/timing, payments/money
2 dates/timing
3 dates/timing, payments/money
4 payments/money

Part B
1 deposit   4 vacancy
2 balance   5 refund
3 fully booked   6 included

Listening 29.3
Part A
Something is …
A damaged
B faulty
D uncomfortable

Part B
damaged "… the plastic panel on the front's broken."
faulty "It's not working properly …"
uncomfortable "… it's blowing out freezing cold air, which is making the room really cold."

Unit 30

Listening 30.1
1 off   4 into   7 downward
2 upward   5 through   8 toward
3 away   6 forward   9 around

Listening 30.2
Part A
Possible answers
1 Asteroids.
2 A situation where most of life on the planet would be destroyed.
3 A rock bigger than one kilometer / two-thirds of a mile.
4 In Hawaii.
5 Photographs are taken of part of the night sky. Then, a short time after, another photo is taken. Then computers are used to compare the two photos and see if anything has moved.

Part B
1 cause   4 make
2 because   5 result
3 due

Listening 30.3
Possible answer
We often say "They" to mean "people in general" or "experts". This differs from the style often used in writing – "It's thought …", "It's not known …" etc.

Solutions to Follow-up Exercises

Unit 16

Follow-up 16.1
Possible answers
1. Electronic books can be downloaded in seconds, so buying is efficient.
2. Storage is efficient, too, because thousands of books can be stored on one electronic device.
3. E-books are better for the environment because they don't use paper, so no trees are cut down.
4. There's no need for transportation, so no CO_2 is produced.

Follow-up 16.2
1 D   2 A   3 A   4 D

Follow-up 16.3
Possible answers
1. The writer disagrees.
2. They predicted that movie theaters would disappear because people would watch movies at home, on video.
3. They predicted that people would buy pop videos and would stop buying music as "sound only".
4. No.
5. People have been able to play video in their homes for over 30 years. So, if they wanted to watch videos instead of reading, why haven't paper books already disappeared?

Unit 17

Follow-up 17.1
1. ring(ing)
2. dial(ing)
3. hang(ing) up
4. cell phones
5. cordless phones

Follow-up 17.2
Possible answers
1. Please hold. / One moment (please). / Just a moment (please).
2. Can/Could I call you back?
3. I'll transfer you. / I'll connect you. / I'll put you through.
4. I'll put Ken on.
5. The line's busy. / The line's engaged.
6. Speaking.

Follow-up 17.3
Possible answers
1. He's organizing a conference.
2. She asked if Adriana could give her some information about the hotel.
3. Because there isn't much information on the website. And she couldn't get through to the hotel using the phone number given on the site.
4. She asked if the hotel has/had a parking garage. Also, she wanted to know whether it's / it was possible to check in during the night.

Unit 18

Follow-up 18.1
1. devices
2. buttons / controls
3. on-off switch / volume
4. manually
5. cable / socket / automatically

Follow-up 18.2
Possible answers
1. You connect the power adapter to an electrical socket.
2. The "charge" light comes on.
3. The "charge" light goes off/out.
4. You have to remove the battery cover.
5. You should disconnect the power adapter.
6. It turns up the sound volume.

Follow-up 18.3
1. When I plug the adapter in , the "charge" light comes on.
2. It's impossible to turn the unit on without the adapter.
3. … when I take the battery cover off after trying to charge it …
4. … should I take the battery out ?

Unit 19

Follow-up 19.1
1. microwave
2. fridge
3. dishwasher
4. paint
5. drapes/curtains
6. wardrobes/closets
7. carpets

Solutions to Follow-up Exercises

Follow-up 19.2
Possible answers
1. They design green spaces.
2. Because, increasingly, plants are used to cover walls and roofs.
3. They look hard and cold.
4. Plants can hide hard materials and give a softer, natural look.
5. Walls covered by reflective glass can be surrounded by trees, bushes, flowers and grass. This greenery is then reflected in the glass.
6. "Greenwall" and "greenroof".

Follow-up 19.3
1 B   2 B   3 A   4 A

Unit 20

Follow-up 20.1
1 C   3 F   5 H   7 G
2 E   4 B   6 D   8 A

Follow-up 20.2
1 fast   4 easily   7 carefully
2 regularly   5 hard
3 well   6 gently

Follow-up 20.3
Possible answers
1. One that used to be difficult and dull.
2. They used to work very hard at home.
3. They used to be very basic.
4. It says that people didn't use to have much free time.
5. Many women with children never used to have any spare time at all.

Unit 21

Follow-up 21.1
Possible answers
1. Because the runway is closed due to snow.
2. Because it's not giving information about the length of the delay.
3. Go home and come back tomorrow.
4. Because it's not certain that she won't be able to fly later today.
5. She doesn't think she'll be able to fly because it's snowing hard. It seems that things are getting worse, not better.

Follow-up 21.2
1 about / having   3 about / solving
2 don't / have   4 could / use

Follow-up 21.3
1 F   3 F   5 T
2 T   4 T   6 T

Unit 22

Follow-up 22.1
1. food
2. the economy
3. recreation
4. pollution
5. climate
6. public transportation
7. education
8. real estate

Follow-up 22.2
1. anything
2. nowhere
3. something / somewhere
4. nothing
5. somebody
6. anybody
7. nobody
8. anywhere

Follow-up 22.3
Possible answers
1. To bring in tourists. And to attract new residents or businesses.
2. That it's the best at something, there's something unique about it.
3. "The gastronomic capital of India."
4. "Unique Selling Point". It means something that's original – a unique advantage that can be used in marketing material to help to sell something.

Solutions to Follow-up Exercises

Unit 23

Follow-up 23.1

Possible answers

1. Excuse me? / Sorry? / Pardon me?
2. You're welcome.
3. Excuse me.
4. No problem.
5. Sorry I'm late.
6. See you later.
7. Thanks a lot. / Thanks very much. / Thank you very much.
8. After you.

Follow-up 23.2

1. I wonder if/whether you could give me a bit of advice?
2. I wanted to ask you if/whether you could give me a few tips.
3. Can you tell me if/whether I should bow?
4. I'm not sure if/whether it's better to just shake hands and avoid the problem.
5. Do you know if/whether that's acceptable for Westerners?

Follow-up 23.3

Possible answers

1. They're examples of cultural groups.
2. In different cultures, people's characteristics are judged differently.
3. People think the employee is quiet and not very friendly.
4. People think the employee is rather silly.
5. They might say the person is boring.

Unit 24

Follow-up 24.1

1. exclusive restaurant
2. food court
3. self-service buffet
4. takeout
5. snack bar, fast-food outlet

Follow-up 24.2

Possible answers

1. explain what's in them
2. seafood
3. vegetarian dish
4. spicy
5. green, red or yellow

Follow-up 24.3

No model answers possible

Unit 25

Follow-up 25.1

1. 50% off / Half-price / Buy one get one free
2. Sale / Special offer
3. Free gift

Follow-up 25.2

Possible answers

1. Because "salesperson" is an unloved job title.
2. They can explain technical information about products.
3. Because sales staff sometimes earn higher commissions for selling some products, so they might try to sell the product that will pay the highest commission, rather than the one that's best for the customer.
4. It's dangerous to see a commercial salesperson as an independent advisor.

Follow-up 25.3

No model answer possible

Unit 26

Follow-up 26.1

Possible answers

1. A run on a bank is when panicking customers withdraw their savings, in cash, from a bank because they're afraid the bank will go bankrupt.
2. Subprime is a term used by banks to describe customers with a low credit rating – that is, people who have a high risk of not repaying their loans.
3. Foreclosure is when a bank seizes a person's home because the person can't keep up their mortgage repayments.

Follow-up 26.2

1. sold / paid
2. bought / cost
3. lent
4. shot / rose
5. withdrew
6. burst
7. fell
8. spent
9. lost
10. won

Solutions to Follow-up Exercises

Follow-up 26.3
1 T   3 T   5 F
2 F   4 T   6 F

Unit 27

Follow-up 27.1
1 Scared to death.
2 When people are frightened.
3 It increases their strength.
4 After physical activity.
5 A feeling of happiness.
6 They feel proud of themselves.

Follow-up 27.2
1 disappointing   4 embarrassed
2 annoying   5 annoyed
3 disappointed   6 embarrassing

Follow-up 27.3
1 too   4 But/However
2 So   5 also
3 But/However

Unit 28

Follow-up 28.1
1 satellite / cable   5 game shows
2 broadcast   6 comedy
3 news   7 documentary
4 movies

Follow-up 28.2
1 F   3 F   5 T
2 T   4 F

Follow-up 28.3
Possible answers
1 It must tell a good story.
2 From a novel.
3 He or she should change as a result of relationships and experiences.
4 A script.
5 The director.
6 They're good for marketing – they help to pull in big audiences.

Unit 29

Follow-up 29.1
Possible answers
1 The plane could land there. And there's a demand for overnight accommodation at the airport.
2 Only one room – the honeymoon suite – has its own bathroom. For guests staying in the other rooms, there are separate bathrooms.
3 The overhead luggage compartments are used as wardrobes. The receptionists wear retro airline uniforms. And breakfast is served on a small tray, like an in-flight meal.

Follow-up 29.2
A 3   C 5   E 2   G 4
B 1   D 6   F 8   H 7

Follow-up 29.3
1 missing   4 faulty
2 dirty   5 unsafe
3 damaged   6 uncomfortable

Unit 30

Follow-up 30.1
1 through   3 away   5 across
2 up / into 4 out   6 around

Follow-up 30.2
Possible answers
1 They're caused by meteoroids – small pieces of rock from space.
2 As a result of the sun's gravity.
3 Because of the meteoroid's speed, it compresses the air in front of it with huge force. This causes the air to heat up to an extremely high temperature.
4 Due to the heat of the air, the meteoroid glows white hot.
5 Many meteoroids burn up completely. But some survive and fall to earth.

Follow-up 30.3
1 400 billion   5 170 billion
2 4.2   6 1 trillion
3 8   7 3 trillion, trillion
4 25,000

Solutions to Language Practice Exercises

Unit 16

Language Practice 16.1
1 my opinion
2 say
3 sure
4 not sure
5 of view
6 as well

Language Practice 16.2
1 I totally agree.
2 I agree.
3 I'm not sure I agree.
4 I don't really agree.
5 I disagree.
6 I totally disagree.

Language Practice 16.3
1 She said she had an appointment in the morning.
2 She said she liked the idea.
3 She said she was busy at the moment.
4 She said she was thinking about the idea.
5 She said she could come to the party.
6 She said she would phone soon.

Unit 17

Language Practice 17.1
1 make
2 mobile/cell
3 give
4 cordless
5 dial
6 hang
7 ringing

Language Practice 17.2
1 Can/Could/May
2 speak
3 moment/minute/second
4 transfer/connect
5 busy/engaged
6 hold
7 call/phone/ring
8 back

Language Practice 17.3
1 He asked where the restaurant is/was.
2 He asked if/whether the store is/was open.
3 He asked when the store closes/closed.
4 He asked how the machine works/worked.
5 He asked if/whether the room has/had a phone.

Unit 18

Language Practice 18.1
1 electricity
2 remote control
3 socket
4 volume
5 button
6 plug
7 cable
8 automatic

Language Practice 18.2
1 Turn up
2 Plug in
3 Turn on
4 Put in
5 Take out
6 Turn off
7 Unplug

Language Practice 18.3
1 I'll plug in the TV. / I'll plug the TV in.
2 Turn on the light. / Turn the light on.
3 Could you turn down the volume, please? / Could you turn the volume down, please?
4 How do you take out the battery? / How do you take the battery out?

Unit 19

Language Practice 19.1
1 dishwasher
2 oven
3 microwave
4 carpet
5 drapes
6 fridge
7 wallpaper
8 painting

Language Practice 19.2
1 bricks
2 stone
3 Concrete
4 wood
5 glass
6 roof
7 grass

Language Practice 19.3
1 D
2 A
3 B
4 E
5 C

Solutions to Language Practice Exercises

Unit 20

Language Practice 20.1
1. clean up
2. vacuum cleaner
3. cut
4. sweep
5. throw / away/out
6. ironed

Language Practice 20.2
1. easily
2. fast
3. more quickly
4. harder
5. well
6. better

Language Practice 20.3
1. At school, I used to be good at art.
2. I used to live in that town in the late 1990s.
3. As a teenager, I didn't use to like sports.
4. Where did you use to live during your studies?
5. In my first job, I never used to work overtime.

Unit 21

Language Practice 21.1
1. thing
2. hard
3. impossible
4. will be able to

Language Practice 21.2
1. Shall we go for a coffee?
2. Let's go for a coffee.
3. Why don't we go for a coffee?
4. What about going for a coffee?
5. We could go for a coffee.
6. How about going for a coffee?

Language Practice 21.3
1. I was able to finish the job.
2. We were able to get some tickets.
3. I wasn't able to answer all the questions.
4. They weren't able to find a hotel.
5. I managed to solve the problem.
6. We didn't manage to get there on time.

Unit 22

Language Practice 22.1
1. D
2. F
3. A
4. H
5. B
6. G
7. E
8. C

Language Practice 22.2
1. anybody
2. somewhere
3. nothing
4. nobody
5. something
6. anywhere

Language Practice 22.3
1. museum
2. gallery
3. statue
4. theater
5. concert
6. stadium
7. bar
8. takeout

Unit 23

Language Practice 23.1
Possible answers
1. Excuse me.
2. Thanks. / Thank you. / Thanks very much.
3. Thanks very much. / Thank you very much. / Thank you very much indeed.
4. Sorry? / Excuse me? / Pardon me?
5. Sorry I'm late.
6. No problem.
7. You're welcome.

Language Practice 23.2
1. Do you know where the airport shuttle leaves from?
2. Can you tell me if/whether there's a bank close to here?
3. I wonder if/whether it's possible to have some food?
4. I just wanted to ask if/whether I could use the phone?

Language Practice 23.3
1. E
2. B
3. G
4. J
5. A
6. D
7. H
8. C
9. F
10. I

Solutions to Language Practice Exercises

Unit 24

Language Practice 24.1
1 D 3 G 5 A 7 F
2 C 4 E 6 H 8 B

Language Practice 24.2
1 say
2 kind/sort/type
3 vegetarian
4 soft
5 vegetables
6 fruit

Language Practice 24.3
1 Could you pass me the water, please?
2 Would anybody like some more vegetables?
3 Would it be possible to have some olive oil, please?
4 Would you mind passing me the salt, please?

Unit 25

Language Practice 25.1
1 F 3 B 5 E
2 C 4 A 6 D

Language Practice 25.2
1 Be
2 Make
3 dangerous to
4 Take
5 not to

Language Practice 25.3
1 to grow, to increase, to rise
2 the growth, the increase, the rise
3 to decrease, to drop, to reduce
4 the decrease, the drop, the reduction

Unit 26

Language Practice 26.1
1 borrow   4 account
2 lend   5 repay
3 interest 6 owe

Language Practice 26.2
1 paid   4 cost   7 sold
2 lent   5 lost   8 won
3 bought 6 spent

Language Practice 26.3
1 four hundred (and) fifty-six thousand
2 two million nine hundred (and) twenty thousand
3 eight billion
4 seven point three four
5 two trillion

Unit 27

Language Practice 27.1
1 fantastic   3 pleased   5 brilliant
2 glad   4 funny

Language Practice 27.2
1 disappointed / disappointing
2 annoyed / annoying
3 depressed / depressing
4 embarrassed / embarrassing
5 terrible / awful

Language Practice 27.3
1 too   3 as well   5 either
2 So   4 However

Solutions to Language Practice Exercises

Unit 28

Language Practice 28.1
1. talk show
2. documentary
3. game show
4. drama series
5. comedy show
6. movie

Language Practice 28.2
1. musician
2. singer
3. group / band
4. single
5. album
6. lyrics
7. guitar
8. piano
9. drum

Language Practice 28.3
1. C
2. D
3. E
4. A
5. B

Unit 29

Language Practice 29.1
1. pitch
2. front desk
3. full-board
4. dining
5. guests
6. lobby

Language Practice 29.2
1. online booking
2. booking confirmation
3. deposit
4. balance
5. No vacancies
6. check out
7. refund

Language Practice 29.3
1. dirty
2. missing
3. damaged
4. unsafe
5. uncomfortable

Unit 30

Language Practice 30.1
1. up
2. out
3. across
4. around
5. away
6. down
7. into
8. through

Language Practice 30.2
1. The highway was closed because of snow.
2. Many people lost money as a result of the stock market crash.
3. The breakdown was caused by dirt in the car's gas tank.
4. There were traffic jams due to roadwork.
5. The virus caused the computer to crash.

Language Practice 30.3
1. It's estimated that there are billions of galaxies.
2. It's thought that there are over 200 billion stars in the Milky Way.
3. It's not known how big the universe is.

Solutions to Extra Practice Exercises

Unit 16

Part A
Possible answer
Sometimes people say they disagree politely and sometimes directly.

Part B
1 disagreement
2 sure
3 agree
4 say
5 view

Part C
C → A → B

Part D
1 B
2 A
3 C
4 A
5 B

Part E
No model answer possible

Unit 17

Part A
1 cell
2 cordless
3 ring
4 make
5 text
6 call
7 answer
8 busy
9 message
10 back

Part B
1 cordless phone
2 ring
3 text message
4 busy
5 voicemail

Part C
No model answer possible

Unit 18

Part A
1 button
2 electricity
3 charge
4 battery
5 plug
6 socket
7 remove
8 replace

Part B
1 T
2 F
3 F
4 F
5 T
6 F

Part C
1 off
2 on
3 to
4 in

Part D
No model answer possible

Unit 19

Part A
1 simple
2 windows
3 dark
4 steel
5 roof
6 bright

Part B
a plastic bottle + some water + some bleach + some waterproof tape

Part C
1 ~~doors~~ windows
2 ~~dark~~ bright
3 ~~walls~~ roofs
4 ~~concrete~~ steel
5 ~~glass~~ plastic

Part D
No model answer possible

155

Solutions to Extra Practice Exercises

Unit 20

Part A
1. better
2. more cheaply
3. more cleverly
4. more quickly
5. harder
6. faster
7. less fairly
8. less safely

Part B
1. dangerously
2. well
3. badly
4. fast
5. hard

Part C
No model answers possible

Unit 21

Part A
1. trouble
2. hard
3. could
4. idea
5. manage
6. difficult
7. sounds
8. how
9. what

Part B
C → D → A → E → B

Part C
Explaining a problem:
1A The trouble is, it's hard to find a time when everyone is available.
2C Unfortunately, I didn't manage to talk to all my colleagues about the idea yesterday.
3C As always, it's difficult to catch everyone together!

Making a suggestion:
4A I guess we could have a meeting without everyone there?
5E Instead of holding a face-to-face meeting, how about having a video conference?
6E So what about doing that instead?

Accepting a suggestion:
7B That sounds like a good idea.
8D That sounds good.

Unit 22

Part A
Group 1: A, D, I
Group 2: B, E, J
Group 3: C, F, H
Group 4: G, K, L

Part B
Possible answers
Group 1: crime
Group 2: economy
Group 3: health
Group 4: education

Part C
1. student / somebody
2. college / somewhere
3. jail / somewhere
4. Drugs / something
5. unemployed / somebody

Part D
No model answer possible

Unit 23

Part A
1. Can you tell me if/whether there are any restrooms on this floor?
2. Could you tell me which floor the restaurant is on?
3. I need to know where the nearest subway station is.
4. Do you know what time the first airport bus leaves?
5. Can you tell me where I can get a taxi?
6. I'd like to know if/whether my colleagues have arrived yet.

Part B
1. Excuse me. / Pardon me.
2. Sorry? / Excuse me? / Pardon me?
3. Excuse me.
4. After you.
5. You're welcome.

Solutions to Extra Practice Exercises

Unit 24

Part A
1 bar
2 cook
3 meals
4 menu
5 served
6 order
7 kitchen
8 bill
9 pay
10 tip
11 waiter
12 restaurant

Part B
1 T
2 F
3 F
4 F
5 T

Part C
No model answer possible

Unit 25

Part A
1 advertising
2 ads/adverts/advertisements
3 advertised
4 advertise
5 risen
6 fell
7 fallen
8 rise
9 fall
10 rose

Part B
1 T
2 F
3 F
4 T
5 T
6 F

Part C
No model answers possible

Unit 26

Part A
1 earn
2 savings
3 withdraw
4 estate
5 market
6 over
7 sold
8 almost
9 cash
10 account

Part B
1 777
2 11,000
3 150,000
4 25
5 290,000

Part C
1 seven hundred (and) seventy-seven
2 eleven thousand
3 one hundred (and) fifty thousand
4 twenty-five
5 two hundred (and) ninety thousand

Unit 27

Part A
1 disappointed
2 terrible
3 However
4 Also
5 annoying
6 So
7 either
8 glad
9 awesome
10 funny
11 too
12 although

Part B
Review 1: a book
Review 2: a DVD/video

Part C
Review 1: [1] [2]
Review 2: [1] [2] [3] [4]

Part D
1 T
2 F
3 T
4 T
5 F

Part E
No model answer possible

Solutions to Extra Practice Exercises

Unit 28

Part A
1 documentary
2 program
3 movie
4 story
5 character
6 actor
7 play
8 part
9 writer
10 script

Part B
1 Both
2 Both
3 Docudrama
4 Docufiction
5 Both

Part C
1 writer
2 actors/characters
3 story
4 documentary/docudrama/docufiction
5 Fiction

Part D
No model answer possible

Unit 29

Part A
1 uncomfortable
2 accommodation
3 advance
4 check
5 vacancies
6 beds
7 desk
8 luggage

Part B
Possible answers
1 comfortable
2 room
3 quiet
4 secure
5 luggage

Part C
No model answers possible

Unit 30

Part A
1 up
2 over
3 away
4 as
5 below
6 around
7 of
8 to
9 on
10 down
11 off
12 through

Part B
1 F
2 F
3 F
4 T
5 F
6 T

Part C
Possible answers
1 the very cold temperature
2 the thick atmosphere / weak gravity
3 the long distance
4 its atmosphere / large lakes of liquid

158

Irregular Verbs

Present	Past Simple	Present Perfect
beat	beat	beaten
become	became	become
begin	began	begun
bet	bet/betted	bet/betted
bite	bit	bitten
bleed	bled	bled
blow	blew	blown
break	broke	broken
bring	brought	brought
build	built	built
buy	bought	bought
catch	caught	caught
choose	chose	chosen
come	came	come
cost	cost	cost
cut	cut	cut
dig	dug	dug
do	did	done
draw	drew	drawn
drink	drank	drunk
drive	drove	driven
eat	ate	eaten
fall	fell	fallen
feed	fed	fed
feel	felt	felt
fight	fought	fought
find	found	found
fly	flew	flown
forbid	forbade	forbidden
forget	forgot	forgotten
forgive	forgave	forgiven
freeze	froze	frozen
get	got	got/gotten
give	gave	given
go	went	gone
grow	grew	grown
hang	hung/hanged	hung/hanged

Present	Past Simple	Present Perfect
have	had	had
hear	heard	heard
hide	hid	hidden
hit	hit	hit
hold	held	held
hurt	hurt	hurt
keep	kept	kept
kneel	knelt	knelt
knit	knit/knitted	knit/knitted
know	knew	known
lay	laid	laid
lead	led	led
leave	left	left
lend	lent	lent
let	let	let
light	lit	lit
lose	lost	lost
make	made	made
mean	meant	meant
meet	met	met
mow	mowed	mown/-ed
pay	paid	paid
put	put	put
read	read	read
ride	rode	ridden
ring	rang	rung
rise	rose	risen
run	ran	run
say	said	said
see	saw	seen
sell	sold	sold
send	sent	sent
set	set	set
sew	sewed	sewn
shake	shook	shaken
shine	shone	shone
shoot	shot	shot

Irregular Verbs

Present	Past Simple	Present Perfect
show	showed	shown
shut	shut	shut
sing	sang	sung
sink	sank	sunk
sit	sat	sat
sleep	slept	slept
slide	slid	slid
speak	spoke	spoken
spend	spent	spent
spin	spun	spun
spit	spat	spat
stand	stood	stood
steal	stole	stolen
sting	stung	stung
strike	struck	struck

Present	Past Simple	Present Perfect
sweep	swept	swept
swell	swelled	swollen
swim	swam	swum
take	took	taken
teach	taught	taught
tear	tore	torn
tell	told	told
think	thought	thought
throw	threw	thrown
understand	understood	understood
wake	woke	woken
wear	wore	worn
win	won	won
write	wrote	written

To be (irregular)

present	past	past question	past negative
I am	I was	Was I …?	I wasn't
you are	you were	Were you …?	you weren't
he is	he was	Was he …?	he wasn't
she is	she was	Was she …?	she wasn't
it is	it was	Was it …?	it wasn't
we are	we were	Were we …?	we weren't
they are	they were	Were they …?	they weren't

To go (irregular)

Questions and negative answers are like regular verbs. Example: to go.

present	past	past question	past negative
I go	I went	Did I go …?	I didn't go
you go	you went	Did you go …?	you didn't go
he goes	he went	Did he go …?	he didn't go
she goes	she went	Did she go …?	she didn't go
it goes	it went	Did it go …?	it didn't go
we go	we went	Did we go …?	we didn't go
they go	they went	Did they go …?	they didn't go

Index

A

a	1
a bit	48
a bit of	48
a few	2
a little	48
a lot	26
a lot of	2
able, to be	2
about	1, 36
above	36
abroad	41
absolutely	2
accept, to	2
acceptable	48
access, to	14
accidentally	47
accommodation	87
accordion	101
account	69
across	53
action	7
activity	75
actor/actress	82, 101
actually	7
ad	36
adaptation	81
adapter	14
add, to	88
address	2
adrenaline	75
adrenaline-powered	75
adult	76
advance	48
advanced booking	88
advantage	1
advertise, to	63
advertisement	63
advertising	63
advice	48
advise, to	53
advising	60
advisor	60
affect, to	48
afraid	8
after	14
After you	47
afternoon	47
afterwards	75
again	19
age	81
ago	7
agree, to	2
air	36
air traffic	36
air travel	36
aircraft	36
airline	35
airplane	87
airport	35
album	85
alcohol	67
alcoholic drink	57
alive	75
all	2
allow, to	13
almost	42
already	2
also	1
although	7
altitude	36
altogether	60
always	14
amazing	93
amused	101
amusement park	76
amusing	101
an	1
analyze, to	41
and	1
angry	76
annoyed	76
annoying	79
another	36
answer	41
answer, to	8
any	26
anybody	42
anything	42
anyway	35
anywhere	42
apart from	94
apartment	70
apologize, to	47
appear, to	20
appetizer	57
appliance	17
appointment	47
approximate	73
approximately	70
architect	20
architecture	20
area	36
around	41
arrangement	91
arrive, to	8
art	42
art gallery	45
article	2
artificially	20
as	1
as much as	76
as promised	76
as a result	26
as a result of	94
as soon as	35

as well	1
as … as …	42
ash	36
ask, to	8
aspect	19
at	2
at all	20
at home	2
at least	48
atmosphere	94
atmospheric	26
attached	76
attachment	8
attention	47
attract, to	42
attraction	45
audience	82
automatic	33
automatically	13
automatism	2
available	54
average	60
avoid, to	1
away	25
away from	93
awesome	75
awful	76

B

back	7
back in	70
backward(s)	93
bad	36
bagpipes	101
balance	88
ballet	67
band	82
banjo	101
bank	69
bank account	69
banking	69
bankrupt	69
bar	45
bare	88
based on	19
basic	26
basin	33
bath	19
bathroom	19
bathtub	33
battery	14
be, to	1
be able, to	2
beat, to	70
beautiful	20
beauty	93
because	2
because of	76
become, to	2
bed and breakfast	87
bedroom	19
before	14
begin, to	69
behave, to	48
behavior	48
behind	94
believe, to	94
bell	7
belong, to	82
below	8
best	36
best, the	42
best-selling	82
better	1
better-looking	20
between	82
beyond	81
big	2
bill	25
bit	48
bite	53
black gold	70
black-and-white	26
blame, to	76
block	82
blockbuster	82
blog	2
blood	75
blow, to	88
boastfulness	42
body	75
book	1
book in advance, to	91
book, to	59
booked	88
booking	88
booming	69
border	81
bored	42
boring	48
borrow, to	69
boss	8
bottom	70
bow, to	48
box	36
break	48
break up, to	94
breakfast	87
brick	20
brief	48
bright	20
brightly	94
brilliant	101
bring, to	42
broadband TV	85
broadcast	101
broadcast, to	81
broaden, to	94
broken	88
broom	29
bubble	70
budget	19
buffet	53

162

building	20	case	20	clear	1
bump into, to	47	cash	69	clear, to	35
burglary	60	cassette	2	clearly	76
burn up, to	94	cause	36	click, to	14
burst, to	70	cause, to	36	client	48
bush	20	caused by	94	climate	41
business	42	celebrity	81	clip	14
busy	8	cell phone	7	clock	82
but	1	century	26	close	20
button	13	cereal	70	close to	2
buy, to	2	certain	35	close, to	70
buying	1	certainly	76	closed	35
buzzword	42	challenging	54	closet	19
by	2	chance	26	cloud	36
by comparison	94	change	2	coat hook	88
by contrast	70	change, to	7	cockpit	87
by far	82	channel	13	cold	20
Bye	47	character	48	collapse, to	69
		characteristic	48	colleague	8
C		characterize, to	82	college	45
		charge	14	color	20
cable	13	charge, to	14	come back, to	35
cable TV	81	charged	14	come on, to	14
cafe	45	chat	48	comedy	81
calculate, to	36	chat, to	48	comment	2
call	7	check	57	commercial	60
call, to	11	check in, to	8	commercialized	42
call back, to	8	check out, to	26	commercials	63
called	94	chef	26	commission	60
caller	8	chemical	75	commodity	70
camp, to	91	chemistry	75	common	26
campground	91	children	26	communication	81
can	1	choice	42	company	41
Can you tell me?	51	choose, to	19	compare, to	70
cancel, to	36	chopsticks	57	compared with	1
cancelation	88	city	41	comparison	94
capital	42	claim, to	59	compartment	87
car	76	classical music	85	complain about, to	76
care	45, 88	clean, to	25	complaint	88
careful	60	clean up, to	25	complete, to	76
carefully	20	cleaner	26	completely	2
carpet	19				

complex	33
complexity	13
complicated	13
compliment	54
component	14
comprehension	54
compress, to	94
concept	81
concert	45
concrete	20
condition	59
conference	8
confirm, to	35
confirmation	88
confuse, to	60
confusing	7
congestion	36
connect, to	8
connection	87
constantly	7
consultant	60
consulting	41
consumer	13
contact	14
contain, to	2
content	2
continually	54
continue, to	2
contrast	70
contrast, to	79
control	13
controlling	17
conventional	87
conversation	48
converted	87
cook, to	19
cordless phone	7
corner	19
correct	48
cost of living	67
cost, to	70

could	2
couldn't	29
country	48
couple	8
course	19, 53
court	53
cover	14
cover, to	20
covered	20
crack jokes, to	48
crazy	70
credential	42
credit	69
credit card	88
crime	41
crisis	69
criticize, to	76
cruise	59
crystal	69
cultural	42
culture	48
culture shock	54
cup	57
current	42
currently	8
curry	54
curtains	19
customer	60
customer advisor	60
customer care	88
cut, to	1
cut the grass, to	25

D

damaged	88
dangerous	60
dark	23
day	2
day out	76
dead	14
dead money	70

deal	76
deal with, to	2
dear	8, 75
death	75
debt	73
decade	2
decide, to	19
decision	19
decrease	63
decrease, to	60
deep	94
definitely	5
delay	35
delayed	36
demand	70
demand, to	2
departures	36
depend on, to	48
depending on	42
deposit	88
depressed	79
depressing	26
descend, to	36
describe, to	7
describing	42
design	20
design, to	20
desk	25
dessert	57
detail	53
detailed	36
detect, to	94
develop, to	82
development	82
device	1
dial	7
dial, to	7
difference	88
different	48
differently	48
difficult	1

difficulty	39
digital	81
digital TV	101
dine, to	54
dining room	87
dinner	53
direction	97
director	82
dirty	26
disadvantage	19
disagree, to	5
disappear, to	1
disappointed	42
disappointing	76
disconnect, to	14
disconnected	14
discuss, to	5
discussion	54
dish	57
dishes	53
dishwasher	19
disruption	36
distance	93
distinctive	87
diverse	82
diversity	82
do, to	19
Do you know?	51
doctor	45
document	88
documentary	81
domestic	26
door	47
double	70
doubt	26
down	1
download, to	1
downward(s)	97
dozen	81
draft	88
drama	101
drapes	19
drink	42
drive, to	8
drop	60
drop, to	63
drug	45
drum	82
dry, to	26
dubbed (over)	85
due to	60
dull	20
during	8
dust	94

E

e-book	1
each	48
early	8
earn, to	60
earth	70
easily	26
easy	48
eat, to	53
eating	60
eating out	53
economy	41
education	41
effect	75
efficient	1
e.g.	47
either	79
either … or …	54
electric	82
electrical	13
electricity	14
electronic	1
else	35
email	2
email, to	35
embarrassed	76
embarrassing	79
emotion	75
employ, to	60
employee	48
en-suite	87
end	70
end, to	7
endangered	2
endorphin	75
engine	36
enjoy, to	87
enjoyable	54
enough	36
ensure, to	14
enter, to	7
entertaining	76
entertainment	81
entrepreneur	87
environment	1
especially	13
essential	7
estimate	94
estimate, to	100
estimated	82
etc.	19
evaluate, to	41
even	2
even if	14
even though	7
even when	81
evening	47
eventually	36
ever	82
every	41
everybody	2
everyday	29
everyone	2
everything	42
everywhere	42
evolve, to	7
exactly	35
example	19

exclusive	53
Excuse me	47
excuse, to	47
exhibit	76
expense	82
expensive	76
experience	26
expert	94
explain, to	54
explanation	54
export, to	81
exported	81
expression	47
exterior	23
extract, to	70
extraordinary	70
extremely	75
eye	1

F

facade	20
face	81
fact	2
fail, to	47
fairly	48
fall	60
fall, to	63
falling	70
familiar	87
family	48
famous	81
fantastic	79
FAQ	88
far	82
far away	93
fare	59
fashion	60
fast	26
fast food	53
fast-moving	7
fault	88

faulty	88
fear	75
feature	87
feedback	76
feel, to	42
feel off color, to	70
feeling	75
feet (measure)	36
few	2
fiction	85
field	7
figure	70
file, to	25
fill in, to	42
film	82
finally	36
finance	70
financial	69
find out, to	35
find, to	19
finger	75
firm	41
first	19
fish	57
fit, to	70
flat	14
flight	36
floor	26, 53
flourish, to	20
flower	20
fly, to	35
flying	36
follow, to	2
following	54
food	41
food court	53
for	1
for example	19
for instance	7
for some reason	8
force	94

forecast, to	2
foreclosure	69
foreign	54
fork	57
form	36
form, to	1
fortune	70
forward(s)	97
free	26
frequently	81
fridge	19
friend	48
friendlier-sounding	60
friendly	42
frightened	75
frightening	101
from	8
front	53
front desk	87
fruit	57
frustrating	36
fuel	60
full	82
full-board	91
fully	14
fully booked	88
fun	75
funny	48
further	19
future	1

G

gadget	33
galaxy	94
game show	81
garage	8
garden	20
gas	94
gastronomic	42
gaze, to	93
gel	88

166

generally	69
generate, to	75
gently	26
get, to	13
get bored, to	42
get through, to	7
get to, to	36
ghost	42
gift	42
give, to	20
give a call, to	33
given	8
glad	79
glass	20, 57
global	69
globalization	82
globalized	81
globally	81
glow, to	94
go, to	19
go for it, to	70
go out, to	14
go through, to	14
go with, to	2
going	36
gold	70
golden	20
good	29
Good afternoon	47
Good evening	47
Good morning	47
Goodbye	47
goods	60
government	69
grab, to	13
grass	20
grateful	47
gravity	94
gray	20
great	53
green	20

greenery	20
greenroof	20
greenwall	20
greet, to	48
greeting	47
grip	75
ground	94
group	48, 82
grow, to	63
growing	20
growth	60
guarantee	14
guess, to	8
guest	54
guesthouse	91
guitar	82

H

habit	60
half	26
half-board	91
half-price	59
hand	48
handout	88
hang on, to	75
hang up, to	7
happen, to	2
happiness	75
happy	53
hard	1
hard-working	48
have, to	1
have to, to	19
he	54
health	41
hear, to	47
heat	26
heat up, to	94
heavy	76
Hello	42
help	60

help, to	8
helpful	54
her	8
here	20
hesitate, to	53
Hi	47
hidden	93
hide, to	20
high	60
highly	1
him	8
historian	100
history	70
hit	82
hit, to	36
hold, to	8
holiday	76
home	2
home video	2
homeless	67
honeymoon	87
hook	88
hope, to	8
hospital	45
host	54
hostel	87
hot	14
hotel	8
hour	14
house	70
household	26
how	26
how about	36
how long	35
how much	8
however	1
huge	82

I

I	2
I don't know	51

I wanted to ask	51
I wonder	51
idea	35
ideal	19
if	2
if required	53
if so	19
I'm afraid	8
I'm not sure	51
image	60
imagine, to	48
immediately	36
important	19
imported	81
impossible	14
impressed	42
impression	20
improve, to	36
improvement	63
in	1
in advance	48
in the end	70
in fact	2
in front of	94
in line	69
in my opinion	20
in order to	26
in other words	35
in this case	20
in-flight	87
incident	36
include, to	41
included	57
inconvenience	76
increase	67
increase, to	60
increasingly	20
incredibly	93
indeed	26
independent	60
index	70
indirect	65
industrial	70
information	7
informative	76
insert, to	14
inside	75
instance	7
instant	81
instead	54
instead of	2
instruction	17
instrument	82
insurance	25
intelligent	13
interest	69
interested	42
interesting	48
interior	19, 87
international	41
internationally	54
interview	76
into	14
intonation	47
invent, to	7
investor	70
invite, to	47
iron	2
iron, to	25
irrelevant	82
issue	41
it	1
item	60
its	1
It's said	94
It's thought that	94
itself	42

J

jail	45
jet	36
job	20
joke	48
judge, to	1
judgment	48
juice	67
jump, to	54
just	2
just over	70

K

keep, to	69
keep up, to	69
keep up with, to	54
key	7
keypad	7
kids	76
kilometer	94
kind	2
kitchen	19
knife (knives)	26
know, to	8
knowledge	54

L

land, to	36
landscape	20
language	6
large	19
last	2
last, to	54
last-minute	88
late	8
later	2
latest	35
laundry	25
lawn	23
lawnmower	29
lazy	48
learn, to	54
learning	76
least	48

leave, to	14	
leave a tip, to	57	
lend, to	69	
length	35	
less	26	
lesson	6	
let, to	13	
let's	39	
life	13	
lifestyle	19	
light	14, 20	
light pollution	93	
light up, to	1	
light year	94	
like	1	
like, to	1	
limited	59	
line	8	
link	76	
link, to	79	
little	48	
live, to	19	
living	41	
living room	19	
loan	69	
lobby	87	
local	42	
locate, to	87	
located	87	
location	93	
long	47	
longer	14	
look	20	
look, to	20	
look for, to	42	
look like, to	1	
looked after	42	
looking	35	
lose, to	69	
lot	2	
lottery	70	
love, to	2	
low	60	
luck	70	
luggage	87	
lunch	48	
lyric	82	

M

machine	26
main	41
main course	57
make, to	2, 97
make a phone call, to	7
make sense of, to	13
make sure, to	60
mall	53
manage, to	36
manner	48
manual	33
manually	13
many	8
map	88
market	69
marketer	42
marketing	42
material	20
matter	19
may	20
maybe	8
me	2
meal	42
mean, to	1
meaning	20
meat	57
media	82
medical care	45
meet, to	42
member	88
menu	54
message	35
metal	70

meteor	94
meteorite	94
meteoroid	94
microwave	19
microwave oven	23
might	26
mile	94
mind	94
mind, to	57
minibar	88
minute	36
mirror	20
miserable	76
missing	88
mix	20
mixed with	87
mobile	11
mobile phone	11
model	14
modern	13
moment	8
money	42
month	8
monthly	69
moon	93
more	2
more … than …	75
morning	47
mortgage	69
most	2
move, to	19
movement	97
movie	2
movie star	81
mow the lawn, to	29
much	1
much more	13
mud	76
museum	45
music	2
musician	85

Word	Page
my	2
mystery	93

N

Word	Page
name	54
native	82
natural	20
nature	20
near	53
nearly	70
need	1
need, to	19
needed	54
needs	60
negative	75
never	19
new	19
news	35
newspaper	25
next	2
next to	8
nice	20
night	8
night sky	93
nightlife	42
no	1
no doubt	26
no longer	14
no matter	19
no point	70
No problem	47
no vacancies	101
nobody	42
nobody knows	100
non-native	7
normally	2
not	2
not just … but also …	20
nothing	7
notify, to	88
novel	82
now	20
nowadays	26
nowhere	42
number	1
nurse	45

O

Word	Page
objective	41
observable universe	94
observe, to	93
obvious	20
obviously	26
of	1
of course	19
off	13, 59
off color	70
offer	59
offer, to	2
office	48
officer	45
often	26
oil	60
old	13
old-fashioned	7
on	1
on the phone	7
on time	47
on-off switch	13
once	48
one, the	7
only	2, 76
open, to	35
opera	67
operation	7
opinion	1
opportunity	70
or	7
orbit, to	94
order, to	53
ordinary	26
organizing	8
original	20
other	35
others	60
our	42
ourselves	75
out	14
out of fashion	60
out of season	42
out of work	45
out-of-use	87
outlet	53
outside	94
oven	23
over	2, 70
overall	1
overcome, to	75
overhead	87
overnight	87
owe, to	73

P

Word	Page
paint	19
panicking	69
paper	1
paradoxically	70
Pardon me	47
park	76
park, to	76
parking	8
parking lot	76
part	82
part, to	47
particular	48
partly	93
pass, to	54
passenger	36
passionately	19
past	29, 93
patient	45
patio	25
pay, to	25

pay in advance, to	91	plug	13	production	70
pay the balance, to	88	plug and play	13	professional	26
pay a deposit, to	88	plug in, to	14	profit	60
payment	69	poem	82	program	81
people	1	point	73	progress	13
pepper	57	police officer	45	promised	76
per	70	polite	47	proof	36
per hour	94	politely	51	properly	26
percentage	82	pollution	41	proud	75
perception	48	pop music	82	provide, to	36
perfect	70	pop star	2	provided	20
period	70	popular	2	public	1
person	48	position	14	publish, to	41
personal	67	positive	75	publishing	1
personality	51	possibility	2	pull out, to	19
phenomenon	81	possible	8	pull in, to	82
phone	7	post	2	push, to	14
phone call	7	poster	82	pushy	60
phone number	8	potentially	2	put, to	7
phone, to	8	poultry	67	put away, to	25
photo	2	power	13	put back, to	17
photograph	26	precaution	63	put on, to	8
phrase	8	precise	73	put in, to	13
physical	75	predict, to	2	put to work, to	70
physically	75	prediction	2		
piano	85	preferably	87		
picture	2	present	93	**Q**	
piece	1	press, to	7	quality	41
pile, to	70	pretty	8	quantity	70
pilot	36	price	59	question	8
pitch a tent, to	91	primarily	82	quick	29
place	19	print	67	quickly	26
plan, to	8	print out, to	88	quiet	48
plane	35	priority	19	quite	76
planet	81	prisoner	45	quite a	48
plant	20	probably	2	quiz	8
plate	57	problem	35		
play, to	2	procedure	69	**R**	
play a part, to	82	process	1	radar	36
please	8	produce, to	75	rain	76
pleased	79	product	60	rain, to	76

raise, to	82
range	53
rank, to	41
rapid	13
rates	69
rather	48
rather than	1
rating	69
react, to	75
reaction	1
read, to	1
reader	1
reading	1
real	20
real estate	41
real-estate	45
realistic	19
reality TV	81
really	42
reason	8
reasonable	93
receive, to	88
receiver	7
recent	60
recently	2
reception	91
receptionist	87
recession	45
recharge, to	14
recommendation	53
record, to	82
recorder	2, 101
recover, to	69
recreation	41
recycle, to	87
red	54
redecorate, to	19
reduce, to	60
reduced	88
reduction	63
refer, to	45
reflected	20
reflection	20
reflective	20
refrigerator	23
refund	88
region	48
regularly	26
related	47
relationship	82
relaxed	48
relaxing	54
reliable	48
remember, to	48
remind, to	2
remote	93
remote control	13
remove, to	14
renovation	19
rent, to	67
repay, to	69
repayment	69
replace, to	2
replacement	14
reply	47
report, to	5
required	53
researcher	100
reservation	88
reserve, to	53
resident	42
respond, to	39
restaurant	42
result	70
retired	87
retirement	87
retro	87
return, to	2
review	2
revolution	2
revolutionize, to	2
ride	70
ride, to	75
right	19
ring	11
ring, to	7
rise	60
rise, to	63
rising	47
risk	69
rock	70, 94
rock, to	82
rollercoaster	70
roof	20
room	19
rough	35
roughly	70
round	7
routine	29
rule	47
rumor	69
run	69
run, to	36
runway	35

S

safe	29
safely	26
salad	53
sale	59
sales	60
sales advisor	60
sales consultant	60
salesperson/salespeople	60
salt	57
same	2
sand	87
satellite TV	81
satisfaction	75
satisfied	79
satisfying	101
save, to	69
savings	69

saxophone	85	
say	42	
say, to	2	
scared	75	
scary	36	
scene	26	
school	45	
science	76	
sciencefiction	87	
score	76	
screen	1	
screen writer	82	
script	82	
seafood	54	
search	14	
season	42	
seat	59	
second language	54	
second (time)	1	
secret	94	
see, to	42	
See you later/soon	47	
seem, to	8	
seize, to	69	
selection	53	
self-service	53	
sell, to	42	
selling	60	
send, to	41	
sense	13	
separate	19	
series	85	
serious	36	
seriously	93	
serve, to	53	
service included	57	
services	14	
set	13	
set up, to	13	
several	76	
shake hands, to	48	
shall	39	
sharp	26	
she	54	
shellfish	54	
shine, to	87	
shock	54	
shoot up, to	70	
shooting star	93	
shopping mall	53	
short	36	
should	14	
show	81	
show, to	14	
shower	19	
shower gel	88	
shy	48	
sign	94	
silently	87	
silly	48	
silver	87	
simple	20	
simplicity	13	
simply	19	
since	7	
sing, to	82	
singer	82	
single	8	
sink	19	
site	8	
site map	88	
situation	88	
size	94	
sized	70	
skill	54	
sky	93	
slip, to	26	
slowly	31	
small	42	
small print	67	
smile	42	
snack bar	53	
snow, to	35	
so	1	
so much	70	
so-called	69	
social	45	
society	59	
socket	13	
soft	20	
soft drink	57	
software	13	
solar system	94	
solution	39	
solve, to	36	
some	2	
somebody	35	
someone	45	
something	42	
sometimes	42	
somewhere	42	
song	2	
soon	36	
Sorry	47	
Sorry about that	47	
Sorry I'm late	47	
sort of	54	
sort out, to	25	
sound	2	
sound, to	26	
space	19, 93	
space rock	94	
spacious	19	
spare	26	
speak, to	8	
speaker	7	
speaking	8	
special	59	
special effects	82	
special offer	59	
species	2	
specific	47	
speed	94	

spend, to	42	stressful	54	tacky	42
spicy	54	strike	36	take, to	2
spoon	57	strong	75	take care, to	60
sports stadium	67	stuck	35	take longer, to	26
sports star	81	student	45	take off, to	14
spring	42	stuff	75	take the opportunity, to	70
squash, to	94	style	82	take out, to	14
squeeze, to	75	subject	2	take time, to	54
stadium	45	subjective	41	takeout	45
staff	53	subprime	69	talent	82
staffed	87	subscribe, to	2	talk show	85
stage	82	substance	75	talk, to	7
stand, to	8, 87	subtitle	85	task	26
standard	88	success	82	taste	82
star	2, 93	successfully	19	tax	60
start	70	such as	1	team	88
start, to	2	suddenly	48	technical	14
starter	57	suggest, to	42	technological	13
static	87	suggestion	36	technology	2
statue	45	suitable	54	telecommunications	7
stay	87	suite	87	telephone	7
stay, to	36	suited	60	telephone, to	7
steal, to	67	summer	42	telephoning	7
steel	20	sun	87	television	81
step	76	support	14	television set	13
step in, to	69	sure	2	tell, to	48
stereotype	60	surely	35	temperature	94
stick out, to	88	surprised	76	tent	91
still	1	surprising	26	term	7
stock market	70	surreal	87	terminology	7
stone	20	surrounded	20	terrestrial TV	85
stop, to	2	survey	41	terrible	76
storage	1	survive, to	54	terrified	101
store	42	sweep, to	25	terrifying	75
store, to	1	swimming pool	70	test, to	54
story	82	switch	13	text	2
stove	91	system	69	than	1
strange	8			thank, to	47
strategy	19	**T**		Thank you	36
street	42	table	53	Thank you very much	47
strength	75	tablet	14	Thanks	47

Thanks a lot	47
thanks to	75
Thanks very much	47
that	1, 20
that's	7
the	1
theater	2
their	2
them	2
theme	2
themselves	42
then	13
there	8
there is/was	1
therefore	60
these	7
they	2
thing	1
think, to	2
this	2
though	7
three-course	53
through	7
throw away, to	29
throw out, to	25
ticket	76
time	2
timing	70
tip	26, 57
tiring	1
title	60
to	1
today	7
together	20
tomorrow	35
ton	70
too	1
top	19
topic	2
total	70
total, to	70

totally	2
touch, to	14
tourist	42
toward(s)	97
town	42
track	101
trade	26
traditional	7
traditionally	20
traffic	36
trail	94
training	88
transfer, to	8
translate, to	54
translation	81
transportation	1
trap	42
travel	36
travel, to	81
tray	57
tree	1
trend	20
trick	26
tricky	19
trombone	101
trouble	35
true	13
trumpet	85
try, to	14
tune, to	13
turn, to	76
turn into, to	87
turn on/off, to	14
turn up/down, to	14
twice	60
type	54
typically	26

U

ugly	20
ultimate	82

uncertain	97
uncomfortable	88
under	14, 88
understand, to	17
understandable	94
understanding	88
unemployment	45
unfair	60
uniform	87
unimaginable	94
unique	42
unique selling point (USP)	42
unit	14
universe	93
unless	35
unlimited	60
unloved	60
unpleasant	42
unplug, to	14
unprecedented	36
unpredictable	54
unpronounceable	36
unsafe	88
until	14
unusual	36
up	1
upgrade, to	88
upstairs	25
upward(s)	97
us	42
use	1
use, to	7
used	8
used to	26
useful	54
useless	70
user	13
using	8
usual	2

V

vacancy	88
vacation	76
vacuum cleaner	29
vacuum, to	25
valuable	60
value	42
vault	70
vegetable	54
vegetarian	54
version	54
very	1
via	70
video	2
video cassette recorder (VCR)	2
view	5
violence	67
violin	85
visible	36
visit	48
visit, to	42
visitor	76
vocabulary	54
volcanic	36
volcano	36
volume	13
voucher	76

W

wait, to	8
waiter	54
walk	53
walk, to	42
wall	20
wallpaper	19
want, to	2
wardrobe	33
wash, to	25
washing machine	26
watch, to	2
water	26
way	26
we	2
wear, to	87
weather	36
website	8
week	2
weight	70
welcome	42
welcome, to	36
well	1, 8, 26
Westerner	48
what	35
what about	36
what if	88
what's more	82
wheat	70
when	2
where	19
whereas	13
whether	5
which	2
while	14
white	26
white hot	94
white-knuckle ride	75
who	41
whole	70
why	2
wide	53
wild	70
will	1
win, to	59
window	25
wire	17
with	1
withdraw, to	69
within	36
without	14
women	26
wonder, to	48
won't	14
wood	23
word	7
work	19
work, to	26
working	48
working money	70
worktop	23
world	41
worry	48
worse	35
worst	41
worth	69
would ('d)	2
write, to	2
writer	85
written	82
wrong	20

Y

year	2
yellow	54
yes	60
you	2
your	2
You're welcome	47
yourself	26

Maps

World

Maps

Europe

British Isles

Maps

North America

Oceania

List of References

Page 87: Jumbostay Pictures (2)
© Jumbo Stay

Page 117: Copenhagen Wheel
© A project by the MIT Senseable City Lab
senseable.mit.edu/copenhagenwheel/
Photos by Max Tomasinelli www.maxtomasinelli.com

Page 177–182: Maps (World, Europe, British Isles, North America and Oceania)
© MAPS IN MINUTES™ 2007